MY SECRET LIFE

W0010579

a truthful look at a child actor's victory over sexual abuse

A Nonfiction/Self-help Book

BY MARTHA NIX WADE

WP Winters Publishing
winterspublishing.com
812-663-4948

My Secret Life: a truthful look at a child actor's victory over sexual abuse

Copyright © 2011 Martha Nix Wade

First printing: April 2011

Unless otherwise noted, Scripture verses are taken from:
HOLY BIBLE, NEW INTERNATIONAL VERSION, ® (NIV), copyright © 1973, 1978, 1984 by International Bible Society. Used by permission of Zondervan. All rights reserved.
Other Scripture is taken from:
A New Translation From the Original Languages, J. N. Darby, 1889 (Darby). Public domain in the United States • The Holy Bible, English Standard Version® (ESV®), copyright © 2001 by Crossway, a publishing ministry of Good News Publishers. Used by permission. All rights reserved.

Published by:
Winters Publishing, P.O. Box 501, Greensburg, IN 47240
In cooperation with:
A Quarter Blue • 146 South Main Street L235 • Orange, CA 92868

All rights reserved. No part of this book may be used or reproduced in any manner whatsoever without written or agreed upon permission of the publisher or author, except in the case of brief quotations in articles or reviews.

ISBN 10: 1-883651-45-X
ISBN 13: 978-1-883651-45-9

Library of Congress Control Number: 2011923123

Printed in the United States of America.

Dedication

For Gary
You are a gift to me!
Thank you for giving me the freedom
to be myself and to tell my story.

Bailey and Ryder
You are my treasures!
May you feel your mommy's love for you.

Points of Gratitude

Thank you to everyone who has encouraged me along the journey of telling my life story. Your words and prayers have been a blessing beyond measure. Thank you to Angela, Bob, Christy, Dave, Erin, Gary, Judy, Meg, Mom, Nancy, Rick, and Wayne for reading the manuscript and suggesting edits. You brought clarity and insight to *My Secret Life*.

The James L. Stamps Foundation, thank you for generously giving a grant to A Quarter Blue in order to publish *My Secret Life*. Thank you for capturing the vision of our mission to stop childhood sexual abuse through education, and to empower survivors to begin the process of healing.

Table of Contents

Introduction..6

Victim

Chapter One - The Innocent...11

Chapter Two - The Predator...19

Chapter Three - The Angry One..27

Survivor

Chapter Four - The Coper...33

Chapter Five - The Lover...45

Victor

Chapter Six - The Forgiver...53

Photo Section...61

Chapter Seven - The Justice Seeker..67

Chapter Eight - The Truth Hunter..73

Chapter Nine - The Woman of Process..81

Brat

Chapter Ten - The BRAT..89

Chapter Eleven - The Unmasked Warrior....................................97

Introduction

I was a bright-eyed, bouncing tow-head whose personality inspired people to talk my parents into taking me to auditions for commercials. One day, my mom drove me to my second audition for a chocolate candy bar commercial. I was elated, not because I was closer to being on television, but because I thought they were going to give me another chocolate bar. I had never experienced the self-indulgent joy of finishing a whole chocolate bar until my first commercial audition.

When the casting director led me into the room, the director had me sit on his lap, to see how I interacted with him. With an innocent openness I asked, "Do you want to see my chickenpox?" as I lifted my dress to show him the rash that covered my legs.

The casting director stormed out of the room straight to my mom, "How dare you bring your daughter to expose all of these children to chickenpox?" Intimidated, my mom replied, "I don't believe it is chickenpox. But I hate to tell you what I think it is," she took a deep breath, "I think she's allergic to chocolate."

Ready to take my hand, and walk me out of the casting director's office with defeated embarrassment, my mom prepared herself to break the news to her four-year-old during an hour and a half drive home.

While the casting director berated my mom, I turned on enough charm to win over the director's heart. He hired me to eat chocolate all day for the camera. And, he paid two grown men to tend to my supposed allergy all day. One held a box for me to spit out each delectable morsel, and the other man wiped my mouth clean of every chocolate remnant. (As it turned out, I did not have a chocolate allergy. Sand fleas were biting me at school.)

In retrospect, this first commercial seems prophetic; my childhood was about masking reality. I got paid, and paid well for appearing to be the flawless child actress. I mastered appearances and faked joy, beyond the camera and behind closed doors. And I became a victim of a sexual predator, who exploited my innocence while I played yet another role, but not for the cameras. I will call him "Uncle" Michael for legal purposes.

Acting became an escape into scripted roles. I got lost in the make-believe—in a world with words and feelings written by adults for me to wear. This was a world made of compliance—a world of hiding my true self. I became the epitome of a child actor.

My publicist, Rod Mitchell, offered me an analogy that seemed to be a word-picture of my life. China dolls appear to be whole on the outside, but are hollow on the inside and so fragile. Their cracks are so fine, and quite often go undetected until they shatter into pieces. As I contemplated this analogy, I went to look at the china dolls in my daughter's bedroom. Was I truly like those dolls on the top of her chest of drawers? They were seemingly perfect, dressed exquisitely, with poised smiles and flawless complexions. That is exactly who I grew up portraying.

Then I noticed one doll which had become sandwiched in between her chest of drawers and bookcase, stuck upside down, just beyond my reach. I took a step back and saw beyond myself and into the heart of molestation. Some victims of sexual assault are like the doll wedged in between the dresser and the bookshelf. Unable to keep up appearances, they retreat, hoping that people will forget that they even exist.

While I did not fall in between the cracks and hide in depression, equally as self-destructive are the dolls "sitting pretty;" they appear unblemished and untouched. This was the character I portrayed most of my life. But if someone had looked in closer they would have seen the vacant eyes, the hairline cracks, and the hollow core. Like these dolls, many victims of sexual abuse maintain their perfect façade, but their inner stability is riddled with fine cracks.

That day, I recognized that I was like a china doll as a child. Many admired, and some envied, the life I led as a child actress. But as I began to face my sexual abuse with truth, courage, and boldness, my china doll-appearance shattered and I started to heal. I began to face the cracks and find authentic beauty, flaws and all—a breakout beauty. I shattered the façade; vulnerable, with tears and humility, I triumphed. I no longer wanted to be a china doll stuck on someone's shelf, collected and admired, but useless. I wanted to dispel the mirage of perfection. I longed to reveal who I was—from the fine cracks to the gaping wounds, so that I could help others. I wanted to reveal the difficulties I suffered as a survivor of sexual abuse so that other survivors would realize they are not alone. As survivors of sexual abuse break out of the silence and shatter the shame internalized for so many years, a true, unexpected, inner beauty will be unveiled.

To those of you who have been violated by another, this book is for you. You are not alone in your trials and pain. We are in this together and I encourage you to see beyond your personal brokenness into a bright world where you claim a life filled with your own breakout beauty. Whether you personally have experienced sexual abuse or another type of brokenness occurred in your life, we all need the tools to become whole again. Much of my courage developed through my understanding of how God treasured me and had amazing purposes for my life beyond my abuse.

I realize the media blots out the faces of children who are affected by child molestation to protect their identities. At the same time many people tend to remain detached, because they have not identified this secret crime with an innocent child. Most victims of sexual assault keep their identities concealed, also. We are rarely given the opportunity to identify with a sexually violated person. As long as society refuses to put a face to molestation, we are crippling our ability to curb the perpetuation of child abuse. Until we know someone who has suffered shattered beauty due to a stone being hurled at his or her innocence, we are unable to feel a passion to awaken the public, the judicial system, parents, children, and other trusted adults to the need to be educated and empowered in the face of a predator.

So, who are we as victims of sexual abuse? While our faces vary in size, shape, and color, our similarities are greater than our differences of appearance. There is no set look to one victimized by sexual abuse. We are white, black, rich, poor, timid, outgoing. I have encountered countless men and women living a life with haunting memories of sexual abuse throughout the world. I am convinced sexual abuse has reached pandemic proportions. Through my experiences with my non-profit organization, A Quarter Blue—Educating~Protecting~Empowering, I have discovered that between 25% to 50% of people within a group have endured sexual abuse prior to the age of eighteen. Recorded statistics are truly unknown, because most victims are afraid to tell or have extreme allegiances to their perpetrator. Victims of sexual abuse feel burdened to keep the secret quiet, often for a lifetime.

I understand wanting to keep quiet. I spent years protecting my perpetrator, afraid that someone would find out our secret. I remained fearful that the truth would erase all the good he had done in the world. His indiscretions could be overlooked, if nobody knew about his secret life with me. I did not want to be the cause of people not benefiting from his kind acts. So, I accepted the position of being a sacrificial lamb. Many of my thoughts were not rational. My feelings would bounce back and forth, contradicting one another. "Uncle" Michael had shaped me into a confused and masked individual over the course of at least five years of sexual abuse. My perceptions were marred by the sexual exploitation and the effects poured out into all areas of my life. For the past nineteen years, I have been committed to unlocking these areas in my life to better understand myself and ultimately to help others. So, today I will share my journey.

This is a story of my life, my secret life.

VICTIM

One who is adversely affected following an egregious act.

CHAPTER ONE

The Innocent

The innocent, trusting, wide-eyed little girl who looked back at me in the photo, had been erased from the timeline of my life. I barely recognized the blonde, blue-eyed little girl as the one whom I felt unable to defend. The words were trapped behind those longing eyes, which screamed for help. The precious gaze came from my own eyes, which looked back at me nearly thirty years later. My mission was for her, not for some faceless frame. My mysterious, painful memories shattered the face I once knew. I needed to get to know that little girl to become the woman I desired to be. I had to reflect back on that helpless, scarred, delicate, fragile face that was me at seven-years-old. Who was I? Why did I fall prey to such a contrived sense of love? How did I survive with all the abuse I had endured?

As I tried to come to terms with my reflection, I was unable to continue with the process of compiling some photos for seminar attendees. I sat before pictures of myself, choking back the tears. I wondered why I had never pictured myself as a child when discussing my victimization. I was flooded with the reality that I was a faceless victim even to myself. While my intent was to show the face of a survivor, to awaken my listeners to the need for awareness and action, I was taken aback when I realized I never pictured myself as a seven-year-old when I described the effects of my own abuse. In trying to alert my listeners to the fact that innocent, precious, trusting children are the face of the abused, I realized that I had never put a face to my own abuse.

Before meeting the man who molested me, "Uncle" Michael,

I was a precious, innocent girl, who longed for affection. One of my few childhood memories is my dad rocking me back and forth in an overstuffed rocking chair while singing "I See the Moon, the Moon Sees Me." I adored my daddy and when I had this one-on-one attention, it filled a special part of my heart. But as I grew up, those memorable times vanished, and I didn't know why. The longing sense of security and love remained, but the opportunities disappeared. As an adult I discovered that my dad's enrollment in a conservative Christian university deeply affected his convictions. The professors seemed to overly focus on condemning outward displays of affection. It was as if my dad was afraid that someone would misunderstand his innocent interactions with me, so he just stopped being appropriately affectionate when I entered kindergarten. However, I had a special place in my heart that then was left vacant. I needed the physical affirmation to assure that my dad loved me.

I believe this feeling was intensified at the age of four when my sister had a baby. I no longer felt like I was her primary source of affection and play. At the same time, another level of stability disappeared when we left one church for another. My parents felt condemned by fellow congregants' judgmental glances and whispers about my sister having a baby out of wedlock. The Sunday following my niece's birth, my dad took me to a growing church in Fullerton, California. He had heard that the senior pastor was a dynamic teacher. This senior pastor, Charles Swindoll, met my dad's expectations. He was a strong biblical teacher, who warmly greeted us and personally led us to the Sunday school class for four-year-olds.

A few months before, we met a leader at that church, Michael. His gregarious, caring personality made my parents feel comfortable. His wife's gentle, sweet spirit seemed to create a harmonious marriage. They reached out like family, encouraging me to call them "Uncle" Michael and "Aunt" Gayle. This remarkable couple served as deacons, second-grade Sunday school teachers, and missionaries. Michael co-founded a reputable missions organization and currently was the support system to missionaries on furlough from their ministries. When my parents joined a missions support group, one of the missionary couples they supported and encouraged was "Uncle" Michael and "Aunt" Gayle.

Over many months, Michael built a perceived trusting relationship with my family. I was one of many children who spent time with "Uncle" Michael and "Aunt" Gayle. It seemed that people within the church felt sorry for Michael and Gayle. They were caretakers of his elderly mom and both of Gayle's aging parents. All five adults lived in their home. People also tried to help fill Michael and Gayle's void, "They love children so much, and yet God hasn't blessed them with children." This led church members to feel they were helping this couple by letting their children play at Michael and Gayle's home. It seemed righteous and safe with five adults watching over us. Also, their home appeared like a haven for children. They had a game room, a pool room, and a yard that looked like an elementary school's playground. While this couple seemed extraordinary, Christians tended to trust other Christians without question.

Around this time I began acting professionally. It became my point of purpose and fulfillment. I did numerous commercials, and at the age of seven I became Mickey and Maggie's adopted daughter, Janice Horton, on *Days of Our Lives* for three years.

Acting became my life, both in front of the cameras and off camera. Most of my days were spent waking up at 4:00 a.m. and riding in the car for two hours to the studio with a guardian. While I was on the soap opera, I loved developing friendships with everyone on the set, from the hair stylist to the cue card guy.

Only once do I remember feeling like a misfit on the set. I had finished shooting my scene and stood by my friend, the cue card guy, to watch the rest of the scene being taped. I was content to be in the presence of a friend. All of the sudden, I heard the snap of someone's fingers. I looked around the studio. My eyes caught the glaring stare down of an actress. She must have thought that we might start talking, so I took a step away from the cue card guy, to remove the appearance of any mischief. In moments, I felt a clutching squeeze around my wrist, as I was pulled away from my friend. My feet were barely able to keep up with the fast-paced strides of the actress. Tears welled up in my eyes from the intensity of her grip. While the shooting continued on the set, the actress began to berate me. I wanted to curl up into a ball, since I did not want to be rebuked for somehow offending her. I was so afraid that I might be blamed for ruining the taping of a scene. I held back the tears, burdened by the growing weight of shame, and sense that I let people down. I did not want to show weakness to this beloved actress, because that might reflect badly on my reputation, so I just took it. How the assault concluded, I do not recall. I learned to keep my distance from this actress. And I constantly discovered ways to keep the peace and make people happy.

I was a child living in an adult world, with adult responsibilities. When my character did not appear in an episode, I had to be in my public school classroom where I felt I didn't have any friends. My friends were in Los Angeles and were three times my age. I felt so alone, and I hated being at school. I would try so hard to fit in, but I was just "the kid on television." I would try to be funny and unique in order to have friends. For a comedic moment, I would pick up something that dropped on the floor and eat it, hence acquiring the name "Martha Midget Mudpie." Not exactly what I was aiming for. Teachers became safe relationships; therefore I would be seen as the "teacher's pet." No matter what I did to build a relationship, I failed. I would hope for more acting jobs, so that I could retreat to where I belonged.

It was when I was aching with loneliness that "Uncle" Michael, my perpetrator, began to violate me. Like most pedophiles, he must have recognized the look in my eyes, the need for a friend and comforter. He capitalized on my tendency to create adult friendships, since they were safe. I willingly played with him and interacted with him in conversation, because he had always been kind and loving.

When given the opportunity to go to "Uncle" Michael's house, I jumped at the opportunity as a child. I was a playful child, but as a working child actress, I had no time during the week for play. Michael would spend all day playing with me. My inherent desire to play was satisfied.

Playing with an adult brought in different rules. My parents brought me up under the realm of absolute rules: "Obey your elders," "Don't talk back," "Never hit." I was the grating child, whose favorite question was "Why?" Explanations were quickly replaced with the repetitious phrase, "Because I said so." Yet I rarely received an answer that fed my curiosity and intrinsic desire to understand the reason behind obedience. I became conditioned at a very young age. I never was given the opportunity to know there were times that I didn't need to follow an adult's requests or demands just because of their age or position of authority. My parents, like many parents, did not weigh the potential effects of quick phrases that implanted half-truths in me.

I have no idea how "Uncle" Michael crossed the line from a seemingly safe friend into a perverse sexual offender. By the time Michael started to make his advances, I knew there was no need to ask why, for it would be, "Because I said so." I was a good, obedient little girl, who did not want to experience anyone's wrath.

But "Uncle" Michael cared about my desires and he aimed to please. He knew what types of entertainment and play were enticing to me. "Uncle" Michael and I would play games, swing and seesaw in his backyard, eat double-scooped ice cream, go to McDonald's for French fries, watch Disneyland's Dancing Waters, and more. So, when sexual acts were the game to receive the reward, I starred in an award-winning performance of "Whatever you say, 'Uncle' Michael." Since I was taught to obey my elders, I did. Seeing that I made my living from following directions, I performed throughout life's awkward moments. No one could see beyond my flawless mirage of the little "television star," who had everything going for her.

"Uncle" Michael knew he had hooked me into a world of silence, appearances, and "trust." He moved in and entrapped me into a life of sexuality, which required performance. I would escape into my surroundings, so as not to remember what was happening to my body. I would drift into the texture of the nubby, vintage, chenille bedspread, into a place where inner feelings and memories vanished.

This relationship was not only based on sexuality, but also on lies and deceit. Michael masked the abuse in play and imagination. Michael created an exciting process of getting close to me. It happened so subtly that I did not understand the motivation behind the adventurous ride in his camper leading to sexual exploitations. Or the freedom of driving his car while sitting on his lap that covered his sick sexual gratifications. While his position of authority created a deceitful mask, so did his stories of where we were going, what we were doing, and who else would be there. My parents had absolutely no idea that Michael would be the only one spending time with me in private, as his wife slipped away to another room. I cannot remember ever thinking I should tell them something was wrong. Reflecting back on it, Michael's subtle ways made his actions normal in my mind. As a child, I could not process that Michael's display of affection was wrong. I had no understanding of sexual intimacy, so I had no words to explain my disdain for the uncomfortable parts of the abuse.

It seemed that in each of my worlds I was playing a role as an actress, daughter, student, and friend—only the audience changed. As an actress, I mastered the child who took direction well for a favorable outcome on tape to countless fans. As a daughter, I strove to be compliant to my parents. As a student, I built relationships with teachers and got good grades, in order to experience affirmation and adoration from educators and my parents. As a friend, I tried to fit in by doing whatever was asked of me by my classmates. I was an actor playing a role in life, in which someone else told me I was good. I longed for people's affirmation and accolades, so I based my understanding of truth on the response I got from onlookers.

While my experience as a child actor is unusual, it encapsulates a more common experience. Child victims of sexual abuse often confuse truth with lies. Truths and lies became blurred in my mind. It became impossible to distinguish the difference, especially since my childhood profession was built on lies and deception.

While playing television characters can be viewed as making a lie appear like reality, that greater confusion was how fans couldn't separate truth from television. Near the end of my time on *Days of Our Lives*, my character's biological mother, Joanne Barnes, kidnapped her. Janice was taken to Florida to experience the amusement parks, and coincidently our family took a trip to Florida at the same time. A fan stopped us in Florida. Not knowing what to do with the fact that she had come face to face with a child who had been "abducted" by her biological mother, she exclaimed, "Janice, you really are here!" We gingerly explained the reality that I had not truly been hiding out with my television mom, Joanne, in Florida. This adult fan could not wrap her brain around the fact that I was an actor, who had a personal life, separate from my character, Janice Horton. Whether it was her excitement to see a "celebrity" that distorted her perceptions of reality, or that she truly did not understand the difference between television and reality—I do not know. The confusion left me perplexed.

Whether it be people's perceptions or my secret life behind doors, confusion concerning truth was a constant theme in my life. When I started to experience the signs of puberty in seventh grade, I realized I wanted to break free from this confusion. I remember a time when my parents went on a date and I spent the night at Michael and Gayle's home. I was lying on the top bunk bed with my face toward the wall. I hoped Michael would go away, if he believed I was sleeping. I was scared that he would feel the changes in my body. When I realized he wasn't leaving, I disappeared into the shadow that my body cast on the wall.

When my development didn't scare him away, I would create excuses, lies, or diversions to not be "babysat" by "Uncle" Michael. Over time, I became masterful in protecting my body when I was around Michael. I did not want to be in these situations any more. I did not want to be violated any more, and I had a gnawing desire to have real relationships with boys my own age.

While I never received an Emmy for my television roles, I sure should have a mantel-full for all the performances I gave over the years as the naive, unaffected child star.

CHAPTER TWO

The Predator

The smells of intimacy nagged me to flee. The weight of deception weighed heavily on my soul. Were we really practicing and perfecting how to be good wives in our role-playing? Our overtly sexual relationship put me on the brink of ruin. I was done. I was scared.

I jumped out of bed and sat, legs crossed, before a full-length mirror. "Did I have AIDs? What did AIDs look like? Who would help me, because nobody knew my secrets?"

News reports were breaking about the AIDs epidemic. The elementary classmate, who continued to lie in bed following our sexual interactions, had no idea of the battle taking place inside of my head, but war raged in my soul.

I did not want AIDs. I didn't want to die! I wanted all of this to stop! I did not want to be a part of this lie anymore, but at the same time, I did not want to lose one of my only friends.

Out of fear and a looming cloud of shame, I began to plot my escape from sexual interactions with my peers.

I longed to fit in without sexual interactions, yet I had a battle taking place inside of me. I had convictions instilled in me by my parents and church, but my desire to be loved and accepted seemed to scream out for fulfillment, drowning out The Voice of Truth. I was working under the false belief that no one could love me for who I was, and I had to do something to earn love and acceptance.

Sexual acting out was a constant thread woven into my childhood relationships. "Uncle" Michael had implanted a seed of sexuality that took a foothold in my life. My closest friends were also seeking acceptance and didn't get a sense of acceptance without inappropriate physical contact either. We masked it in playing doctor or practicing for our future mate, but it was a skewed sense of reality. I have no idea if any of these kids were sexually abused, but I am confident they were, and somehow we knew how to find one another. I had this type of relationship with a handful of boys and girls. All of them came from broken homes, except myself. I remember feeling trapped, and not wanting to do much of what was being asked of me by the various kids, but I dissociated, so as not to lose the few friends I had. I could not say "No." I felt like a marionette being manipulated by my strings, and I couldn't cut the ties connected to these relationships; they were all I had outside of my work.

One day in school, a teacher confiscated a book that one of my friends and I had made. In stick figures we illustrated sexual acts that we had done and those that were on our "To Do List." My heart beat rapidly, unable to breathe, as my eyes followed the booklet, praying he would throw it in the trash. Each step seemed to take a lifetime as I drowned in the possibilities of what would be my fate. He passed the trashcan and moved to his desk, placing the sex guide into his desk drawer. I am sure the rest of the day was a blur. The terror of having my secret discovered overshadowed the rest of that day's happenings. Days turned into weeks and nothing was ever said. But shame weighed heavily on me. This fear gave me more reason to stop acting out sexually.

Most of my life I believed I remembered each of the children with whom I acted out. That perception crumbled one day when we posted a Croatian interview concerning sexual abuse on a social networking site. A girl I knew in elementary school wrote:

> *Martha, I watched your interview and it brought back a lot of memories. Just before I started first grade (age 5 or 6), I came over to your house ... you took me in the bathroom. I don't really have the words to explain what I remember except to say this is what as*

adults we call "sexually acting out." We were never friends after that. Not that I didn't want to be your friend, but you were popular and I wasn't. I wonder if I had said something then if maybe someone would have seen that something was wrong. My guess is probably not. It seems like people were always looking the other way back then. I was the victim of physical and emotional abuse and in later years there was some sexual abuse by a family friend. When I did first tell my mother she blamed me and I am sure that I am very changed because of it. I have had lots of therapy and I am doing very well, although there are some left over things even now. Anyway, thank you for sharing your story, it helps to make sense of things for me a little bit more. I appreciate your courage and wish you well in all you do."

My heart dropped. I felt overwhelmed with grief that I was not always the one who felt manipulated and trapped. I had also been the aggressor, yet I suppressed memories of my initiating sexual contact. My heart broke, realizing that I had planted the seed of sexuality in other children. Who else might I have forgotten? I needed to start asking her for forgiveness.

Thank you for revealing the truth to me. My memories are next to nothing—except I know I lied and believed I could not have friends without sexual interaction. I AM SOOOO SORRY for initiating that sexual contact with you! Words cannot express how sorry I am. I wish I could take that back. I was sooo confused. I remember a few children I "acted out" with, but I had no idea about you. I am sorry. I am sorry I discarded you, too. That is not who I wanted to be—it is horrible that you felt I was more "popular." I know that many people looked the other way. I'm thankful you have gone to counseling and feel better. If there is anything I can do to help, please let me know! Thank you and sorry again!!!!

With love and humility, Martha

I quickly followed up with another message:

I wanted to add that I am saddened about your mom's

response. Unfortunately, it happens over and over.

Also, we will always be on the path to healing—the web of abuse tangles so many facets of our life. God will reveal different points of needed healing and bring beauty out of all that we work through. I appreciate your boldness in telling me—once again ... sorry.

I began to search myself. It seemed like I became a predator preying on weaker prey—a lesson learned from my perpetrator. I remembered sitting down with a former elementary classmate, hearing about her sexual abuse by a neighbor. I had to wonder if I had initiated the pattern, so I wrote her. Her response caused my heart to skip beats. "Yes, if you want to know details, I will let you know." She described how I imitated sex, yet she graciously forgave me.

If any of these individuals I had inappropriate contact with as a child are reading this book, please forgive me. I meant no intentional harm. I was seeking love and acceptance from my peers, and Michael wrongfully taught me there was only one way for me to be a friend and have friends. And once again, please accept my apologies, for I did not understand the depths of what I was doing. It took me a long time to figure a way to cut the ties of my addiction to sexuality.

It was during this time when I started my work on *The Waltons* as Serena Burton, the troubled girl who moved into the Walton home with her brother and grandma, escaping an abusive father. I was thankful to find fulfillment in my work and not in trying so hard to gain approval from my peers or avoiding Michael. However, I still longed to be loved, accepted, and recognized. I loved going to school with Kami Cotler, who played Elizabeth, and Keith Coogan Richards, who portrayed Jeffrey, my on-stage brother. Our schoolteacher, Glen, provided us with a dynamic learning environment, and poured into our lives intellectually and personally. While Keith and I would sometimes have tiffs like a real brother and sister, we had a good time as our characters got into trouble. Episodes brought on mischievous and exciting antics like stealing a car, bandaging up Keith so he was unable to move, stuffing my bra, and more. Kami was very accepting of me, even though I probably tagged along like a pesky little sister more than she was used to, but she was kindhearted throughout my year on the show and beyond.

Even though I had a retreat from being at school and found purpose in my work, I still longed to stand out and be recognized. The cast of *The Waltons* had many actors, and I needed to find a way to be noticed and adored. Eric Scott, who portrayed Ben, had the record for the most re-takes. Everyone seemed to have a special affection for him, because he could joke about his errors. In the back of my mind, I saw this as an opportunity for acceptance. As we approached Eric's record, I plotted on how I would react when I missed a line. I hoped that if I made light of my mistakes, I would get a laugh. All I wanted was to beat Eric's record by one. I started to sense the brewing anger in the crew, so I began to get scared that the cost for re-shooting was not at all humorous. I have never known why Keith and I were not rehired the following season, but I am sure this ploy did not help. I didn't even realize I was attempting to disguise my pain in overdrive, seeking acceptance and recognition at any cost.

When the season's filming ended in February, I had to return to a public junior high. When I walked through the school doors, the whole school seemed to stand still. In a sweeping motion that seemed to slice through my core like a frigid blade, the students turned their heads to stare at "Serena" walking through the door. I hadn't even decided who was walking through the door and what role I would play to fit in. Before I could remove the dagger that left me numb, I had to put on my actor-face. A few students swarmed around me asking for my autograph, and I didn't know what to do, so I chuckled. "Oh, you don't want my autograph." Oh, great! Did this make me a stuck-up snob? They didn't give up, so I gave in, and quickly wrote my name on the shard of notebook paper. Oh, shoot! Did this make me arrogant? I couldn't win. One kind eighth grader, Jenny, reached out and protected me. "Come on. Share my locker with me." Somehow she got the other students to leave me alone. We shared a locker for that year and developed an appropriate friendship. I had developed a new identity, because she illustrated an unconditional love and acceptance of me. I was very grateful for this healthy relationship during that overwhelming time. However, I became frightened about whom I would transform into without Jenny as my advocate and friend. I became even more fearful when I was not given the opportunity to return to another season on *The Waltons*.

Without being able to completely retreat to a studio on a regular television role, I decided I desperately wanted to get out of my adult-like responsibilities in the acting world; I did not want to be different from my peers.

One day I had to leave early to shoot a commercial with my dad as my co-star. I begged my mom to let me get out of this responsibility, and the business as a whole. She did not believe that was what I really wanted, so she challenged me to call my agent to tell her. I could not do it; I had to please my agent. Feelings of frustration welled up in me. These feelings only amplified when a limo picked me up from home, and it passed right by my junior high. I couldn't sink down low enough in my seat to avoid being seen. Everybody in the limo laughed. The limo driver said that his daughter would be sitting up tall and waving to everyone, if she had that privilege. That was exactly it! I did not want to be "privileged!" At that moment, I believed I wanted to mesh into the crowd and not be noticed. However, when I saw Sammy Davis, Jr. on the commercial shoot, a sense of belonging muted the desire to retreat from acting. I couldn't decide which world I wanted to be in. I just wanted to be able to pick one and not move back and forth between these two worlds. I wanted to land in one place and please the people who were in charge.

Since I didn't have a regular role during this time, I spent most of my time at school. I had to figure out who was in charge and please them. I discovered who had popularity and sought to perform to gain their acceptance. With this desire, I began to try and fit in by pretending to drink at parties, cussing like my friends, forming an "elite" group of friends, and fooling around with guys. When my boundaries got pushed, I would say, "No," and then the guy would try again, so I would laugh, so as not to reject him. I was trying to deter him and play "cute." All the while screaming inside, "STOP!" I wanted more than a physical relationship; I wanted to be loved for who I was. But my voice had been silenced over the years of sexual abuse. I still felt my opinions didn't matter. I falsely believed my convictions would always be in my head, and never in my life.

I knew God was watching my every move, but so were my friends. I perceived God and my parents as my fans. They loved and adored me. They would love and forgive me forever, no matter what. I convinced myself that my friends might reject me like in my early junior high years. For my friends, it was all about image; I believed there was no room for convictions. Three of my greatest fans might be disappointed, but my friends might not be so quick to forgive and forget if I were completely authentic. I didn't care to take the risk. I was finally popular and that was all that seemed to matter. I would spend the night at someone's house, and then we would sneak out to parties or meet boys. When we went to parties, I tried drinking, but I hated it. The taste grossed me out. And I absolutely hated not being in control of my behavior. So, I became a poser drinker. I kicked in my acting abilities and pretended I was drunk. I thought that this was what everybody wanted. I thought this was normal, and I went along with the flow.

My freshman year in high school, my group of friends upped our exclusivity. We were mean to girls who did not fit our visual expectations. We shoved rotten bananas in an innocent girl's locker to move her out and claim our territory. She soon could take no more of our evil pranks and comments, and relocated her locker and made new friends. I wish I could tell her how sorry I am. She was a kindhearted girl who had her one-time friends turn on her out of conceit.

For one who had grown up being bullied, you would think I would have stopped these heartless acts, but I had convinced myself that popularity had its price. And while I couldn't control my friends and what they deemed acceptable, I was bound and determined not to be the victim here. So, I took my own personal pain and used it to hurt others who were just trying to be authentic.

And I still sought out approval from guys through being physical with them while dating. The one relationship I treasured, I severed because my friends disapproved of our relationship. They told me I had to choose between my dating relationship or them. In fear that I'd lose my friends, I broke it off. I found myself crying on and off throughout my high school years. He was one guy who did respect my boundaries.

For some reason, no guy ever pushed me to the point of having sex. This was a total Godsend. While my heartfelt desire was to wait to have sex with my husband, I was not equipped to stand up for my convictions. If I had been pushed that far, I wouldn't have had the courage to go against the wishes of others.

The winter of 1981, I realized how twisted I had become. I had gotten away from the foundation that my parents had established in my childhood, to love others despite their looks.

A night at high school church camp changed my life. The speaker asked if we were part of a group that ostracized kids. I thought to myself, "No way, not us! Everyone hangs around us!" A spotlight then illuminated the depravity of my soul. I realized I had become an arrogant, haughty follower. Nobody forced me to be a mindless puppet, but I was compelled to do so with a robotic obedience that I had mastered in Michael's camper, pool, and house. I turned off reason and honor, in exchange for acceptance. I had sold out!

A list of my victims flashed before me. I woke up to the fact that I did not like the person I had become. I was broken, with true humiliation and humility. I wanted to break down the walls that created an unhealthy façade. I wanted to reach out to people, regardless of their level of popularity. I wanted to develop healthy relationships, without expecting anything in return, and not compromise my personal convictions. I did not want to be tangled in the messy weave of the life I had created. I no longer wanted to be a victim or victimize others. I wanted to live a life driven by the convictions in my heart—not afraid of them.

In many ways I grew up guarded. Strict rules and expectations made me fearful of feeling too deeply or expressing my emotions inappropriately.

CHAPTER THREE

The Angry One

"You are angry. Your anger begins to bubble at the pit of your stomach, like bubbles created in a shaken bottle of Coke, but the anger is trapped in the glass and imprisoned by the bottle cap. Your anger gets more and more shaken inside of you and it wants to burst. But the cap keeps that anger trapped. You are so angry that you are about to burst, but you hold back," bellowed my acting teacher.

Each step, I closed my eyes even tighter, digging into my soul, trying to identify with the emotion of anger my acting teacher was leading us through. "... And then, you feel it, the cap is cracked, and you spew a little ... and then ... POP!"

I wanted to have an authentic, visual response that pleased my acting teacher. When I tapped into what I thought was as deep as I could go, there was nothing, for anger was an emotion that I was never allowed to have. Anger was "a sin." So, cautiously I peeked through one eye, squeezing the other even tighter, so as to not get caught. I needed to cheat off of another child actor to see what true, growing anger looked like. One day I mastered this learned expression ... I had succeeded in pleasing him! I acted angry!!!

Still, true anger, justifiable anger, remained trapped in the bottle inside of me. I felt no available outlet, so subconsciously I went to work. I gnawed on the ridges on the inside of my cheeks, holding onto the secrets I felt forced to repress, which created permanent scarred ridges. I also developed temporomandibular joint disorder, TMJ, from constantly grinding my teeth in the night, attempting to work out the pain, confusion, and shame, since I had to be "on" as the "child star" when I was awake.

Countless survivors have shared medical problems, which I believe are directly connected to their abuse. Our trauma has played out in our bodies. Each of us has reason to rage, but instead we store the turmoil and our bodies inevitably break down from the unaddressed pain and confusion. For me, I had to suppress my emotions, so as not to destroy my image as a good, little, compliant Christian girl. So, I continued to play the role into high school.

I had been working on a sit-com for about nine months my senior year of high school. During much of that time, it was just part of the job to endure unwanted sexual innuendoes and touching. This was seen as playful interaction for many people on the set. I usually played along, just as I had seen most actors do throughout my career. But something snapped in me, the cork on my bottle spewed, when an executive on the production was showing executives from the station around our set. He grabbed my butt, just like he always did, but I had had it. I was fed up with his inappropriate way of displaying his control over us. My defensive nature lashed out, something I didn't even know I had deep inside, but I had to temper it with a slight comedic edge to keep them guessing... Did she really mean that? Within the split-second I delivered my line, "Take your hands off of my rear-end. There's my teacher."

My studio teacher was supposed to be my advocate if anything illegal took place on the set. But he remained silent. Unfortunately, the times were different, and it was not popular or politically correct to report sexual harassment. This happened before the infamous sexual harassment case of Anita Hill verses Clarence Thomas. My friend jokingly says, "Too bad you were sexually harassed before your time."

However, this was no joke. A few weeks after this incident and my eighteenth birthday, I was fired. It was blamed on my acting. The executive said that the editor had to edit scenes around me to save the show. The timing was all too suspicious.

The actors' union admitted we had no recourse; they had missed some loopholes in my three-year contract when it was approved a year earlier. I did not know where to turn. My friends were all at college, at least an hour away. I was in a condominium with no job to pay the bills, and a reputation that had just been seemingly shattered by the slip of the tongue.

I had forfeited my acceptance to UCLA to continue my work. I had missed the start date by one day and did not have the emotional energy to fight the system to see if there was even a chance that I could enroll the day after school started. I could not find purpose with no work and no school. I had no stage on which to perform. I felt defeated and destroyed inside. At the same time, I had to dive into new auditions, to try and open up another opportunity to have a role to play.

While on a callback interview for a new show, I sat before executive producers. One writer/producer asked why I was no longer on my sitcom. I thought to myself, "It pays to be honest, right?!"

I took a deep breath and hoped that God would reward me with this role for being honest, "It looks like I was fired because I told the producer to take his hands off of me."

Who knew that the man who groped me was a close, personal friend of one of the executives at that meeting?! I received a letter from a lawyer to cease and desist. From there on out, the opportunities to work in the television industry nearly vanished. My self-esteem shattered. My purpose disappeared.

The lie instilled by "Uncle" Michael began to replay in my head, "See, you're only valuable to others physically." This inner voice got louder and louder and even more frequent the less the phone rang for auditions. I did not have even the slightest clue I was being influenced by these lies. I did not know I was actually reacting to these false claims. It was almost an impulse. This voice of deception began to murk any clarity I had in my life, any clear sense of purpose outside of my sexuality.

I hit the absolute bottom when militant guerrillas kidnapped four missionaries in Colombia. My junior year in high school, I had worked on a team from church in the jungles of Colombia, building a home for a new pilot who would deliver needed supplies in the depths of the jungles, painting, and learning about various ministries. One of the highlights was when a seasoned missionary pilot flew us to visit a tribe. We were able to meet tribesmen, eat tribal food, and interact with the two missionaries dedicated to translating the Bible into this indigenous language. A year later, the two pilots and this husband and wife were all kidnapped. Our team felt an amazing connection to these people we worked alongside for three months. When news arrived about their kidnapping, I had lost all hope. Why would God allow my life to crumble if it had any purpose at all?

These incidents seemed to throw me into reverse, and I could not shift gears to stop the depression and chaos. One day as I drove on Hilgard Avenue, a curved street adjacent to UCLA, I thought, "If I just drive straight, this will all be over."

At that moment, I sensed a booming voice from above, "I gave you life! What right do you have to take it away?" God had not created me to be destroyed by turmoil; I needed to live above my chaos and confusion.

I did not have a clue how I was going to press on, but a rush of peace overwhelmed me. My broken dreams, expectations, and relationships were not miraculously understood and restored, but I realized that I did not need to understand them. I did not need to be weighed down by not understanding why I was punished for speaking my opinion. I did not need to torture myself for standing up for what I knew was right. I did not need to run from something that seemed insurmountable, for I was not alone.

My pity turned into an aggressive spirit to overcome whatever I had to face. However, I did not realize that deciding to live was just a beginning.

Part of life is learning to express anger. As a child, I was afraid to express how I felt. As a teen, I was punished when I showed justifiable anger. The firing from the sit-com could have led me to believe that I should remain passive and non-confrontational. But I knew instinctively that doing so would lead to a crippled adulthood.

Anger management continues to require constant self-evaluation and humility. How can I find the balance between expressing true emotion and not hurting others? How do I avoid detached passivity on the one hand and senseless emotional outbursts on the other? Will I remember to be sensitive to other people's feelings and apologize if my passion is misinterpreted as unjustifiable anger? I don't want to use my personal pain as an excuse to be angry or to hold grudges. I want my anger to lead to productive action.

SURVIVOR

One who remains alive or in existence.

CHAPTER FOUR

The Coper

My new defense was to help others in any way I could. If I could deny myself and help others, I would feel a greater sense of purpose and satisfaction. Following my awakening that my life was worth living, I plunged into church leadership. I oversaw a group of high school girls. I listened and gave advice, thinking that I had rich life experience to share. I also served on cross cultural mission service trips to Alaska, Papua New Guinea, and Brazil. Our mission teams had great impact on the people we went to serve. However, I did not recognize I was living to serve, yet living a lie. I tried to be selfless and giving of myself. I did not realize that in selflessness I forgot my own needs by attending to the needs of others.

Since I had never looked at my past, I never conquered my tendency for false acceptance. I was not truly equipped to help people or projects. I had never reached into my own soul for authenticity. I did not really understand my struggles concerning my inability to say, "No." I loved serving others, and putting them before myself; I did not want to chance losing my impact in others' lives. Unfortunately, I did not realize I needed just as much help, and that I was living a hypocritical lie.

I was in survival mode. I knew how to exist and shove away my imperfections, but I did not know how to be real with my weaknesses. Sexual molestation had left me impaired. The memories of the abuse were tucked away in the darkness, except for a fragment of truth I revealed to my then boyfriend, now husband, Gary. What little I remembered about my abuse, I told Gary. He had proven to be faithful, and not run away from me embarrassed or ashamed.

In preparation for marriage, we went on a missions trip to Brazil—premarital counseling. I had a longing to work with Brazilian street kids in the arts, but Gary's only "cross cultural" experience was the Canadian side of the Niagara Falls. Doug Haag, my former high school pastor, who led my team to Colombia in 1984, counseled us to go for three months to see how well we worked together with language and cultural challenges. I also hoped Gary would gain a peace about dedicating his life to overseas work. The trip changed our lives forever, not because Gary felt led to serve a lifetime in Brazil, but because my childhood secret became exposed to the light.

Doug sent me a letter, and asked if anyone at the church had ever been inappropriate with me.

"Oh, crap. It came out!"

I felt defeated. I had spent a lifetime dismissing my discomfort and upholding Michael's character. I couldn't lie to Doug, so I called him and shared about my minimal memories. "How did you find out?"

That Sunday the church had an "exemplary" couple (Michael and Gayle) share about their volunteer service to second graders. Another woman who had been molested by Michael sat in the congregation. She gasped, "He's still working with children."

Her husband and she knew they had to tell Doug, who at the time oversaw family ministries. The church had to know the truth about Michael.

She said, "I think there is someone else you need to talk with. In junior high, I saw a photo of Martha Nix in Michael's wallet."

This triggered a sense of regret. Two years prior to this, I was on a different missions trip to Brazil. I was one of four leaders for high school students. I received a letter from Michael that was remarkably encouraging. I began to share the letter with a high school student. She interrupted me, "He grosses me out. He French-kissed my aunt." I found myself scrambling to dismiss her accusation with smokescreens to protect his character and good works.

After recalling this incident, I added, "... And Doug, if that's how you found out about me, you might want to call ..." and I began to name the aunt of the high school student and a couple of other girls who spent a lot of time with Michael during my childhood.

Within weeks, Doug and another associate pastor sought out the truth about this elder, Sunday school teacher, and co-founder of a major missions organization. They did not want to act with haste in accusing Michael of child molestation; they looked for sufficient evidence. Two of the women I told Doug about confirmed Michael's pattern of molestation.

Once they had these four women's testimonies, they confronted Michael. He denied it.

They went to the church counselor. The three of them sat down with Michael, trying to draw the truth out of him. He denied it.

Then the three church staff members went to the senior pastor, Charles Swindoll. While his heart wanted to hold onto disbelief, he knew his thorough, trustworthy staff had revealed the truth to him. The four of them sat down with Michael. Pastor Chuck said, "You are a pedophile. What you did to these girls was immoral, ungodly, and illegal. We have no reason to disbelieve these women."

The church counselor encouraged Michael to write his admittance to be read to the church leadership. The revelation left the elders overwhelmed with grief and uncertainty about the next step. What should they do? How did the law bind them? Should they make this public with the church community?

They decided to follow biblical teaching first, "Those who sin are to be rebuked publicly, so that the others may take warning" (I Timothy 5:20).

The church did not hide in shame, as if it were some reflection on them or on God. They truly lived out the Bible verse, "The truth shall set you free" (John 8:32b Darby Translation). They recognized that even if a man has lived out his life in conjunction with the name of God, that does not make him God. Man is fallible and that does not change the infallible nature of God.

Pastor Chuck spoke boldly from the platform. He removed Michael as an elder and excommunicated him from the church. For the following ten years a team would go to Michael and Gayle's retirement complex and church to let the management and leadership know that they had a pedophile amongst them. Typically they were sent away with, "Leave that poor man alone!"

While we were fortunate for our church to expose the truth, this is not the norm. If Michael's missions organization had been so bold when they discovered the truth, I would not have been one of Michael's victims. In the 1950's, parents representing 50 missionary children went to the board and spoke of Michael's sexual indiscretions with their daughters. The board claimed they would get Michael into counseling and change his leadership position. His new ministry position was to greet and care for missionaries when they were stateside for a year. I remember playing with missionary girls at the local missions headquarters. We also discovered that a report was filed in the early 1960's with the local police department.

Our church focused on helping the victims. The church developed a support group for the women Michael victimized. The Director of Women's Ministries guided us through this vulnerable time in each of our lives. Even though our ages ranged twenty years, we were united through life experience at the hand of a devious man. Our stories unfolded as if there were one author. Michael was a creature of habit. He had mastered the perfect formula to lure in his victims and keep them hooked with rewards and bound with silence in allegiance to him. Our lives had been profoundly impacted, but so many of our memories were gone. We felt if we could remember more of the acts perpetrated by our pedophile, we could better understand why we were the way we were. The church gained access to Michael and Gayle's home, to see if that would trigger any of our memories. I was the only one who had been in Michael and Gayle's home as an adult.

As we walked around their house, no flood of memories came back to us, but we did have confirmation of what we did remember in their home, and had a better understanding of the mind of our perpetrator. Michael and Gayle's single beds with the bumpy bedspreads were still right on the other side of the wall of the piano in the living room. Those girls who had siblings remembered that wall well. One of the girls would sit at the piano bench with Gayle by her side, while the other would be on the opposite side of the wall with Michael. Gayle taught piano, while Michael instructed the other girl in the ways of sexual intimacy.

All of us remembered the sign, which read "Lar Doce Lar," "Home Sweet Home" in Portuguese. We were able to laugh at the irony of that posted sign being one of the only things we recalled, before Michael drew us into his perversion. How many times did I read "Lar Doce Lar," trying to escape the reality of what was happening to me?

Many of us went to the camper parked in the driveway. The doggy chew toy still kept the door shut. If we could have opened the door, would his insidious acts come flooding back, and help us through our healing?

Throughout their house we found pictures of little girls. We were able to identify many of the girls who grew up at church with us. We saw our photos on Michael and Gayle's walls and in their photo albums.

Spread out on their dining room table were letters from many friends of theirs stating: "We know you are innocent;" "Who could accuse you of such heinous acts when you have done such good?" "We know these girls are lying!" Michael and Gayle also had a phone log of each call that had come in since his excommunication, and what each caller had stated. The point that aggravated us the most was that people who were defending Michael had children who we believed were victimized by him.

We felt for those girls. We had each other to validate our feelings, our disconnected memories, and encourage us in the process of healing. Who did they have? Was their secret trapped behind lies and fear? They must have felt immense betrayal. Their parents' defense of Michael did not give them security in speaking out about what happened to them. They were already being told that family members would not believe them. "He is innocent because of all the good he has done in the name of the Lord."

How brazen! How ignorant! How infuriating! Michael and Gayle had people buying into their masquerade. Unfortunately, this is normal. People trust "beautiful benefactors." They back up men and women in positions of authority. Typically, pedophiles mask their addiction behind their title and good works, in hopes that it will be an effective mirage— and typically, it works.

We had mixed emotions, leaving that night. We wanted to address our scars. We had hoped uncovering lost memories would help unlock the gate to our wounded hearts. But nothing came into focus from our past. We left with the same vacancy of memories floundering in the abyss. We had to face the fact that memories of the past may not be part of the healing process for each one of us.

Instead of focusing on the abuse itself, we had to go back to looking at the effects of abuse.

As a teen, I tried to build life on academic success, alcohol, friendships, and serving others. Each left me with untended wounds that scarred over; each left me with an insatiable vacuum at my core. I realized that this emptiness could not be filled until I faced my own internal brokenness the abuse left behind.

Was I willing to admit I had brokenness in my life, after living for accolades of perfection my whole life? Could I extinguish the lies that became truth in my head through a fake grin, a witty humor, or a "just accept me as I am" attitude? I felt I didn't have a choice. Gary and I were preparing to be married and I wanted a marriage that was built on truth, not on deceit and appearances.

Determined to be healed, I dove into a year-long commitment to counseling. Two days a week, Gary would go to a men's group. I would go to my survivors' group on the same night. My parents went to a parents' group. One day a week, I would see a professional counselor the church was able to arrange through a financial trust, as part of Michael and Gayle's restitution agreement. In one year, we would all be healed and knowledgeable about sexual abuse.

WOW—was I disillusioned! I could not control the length of time it would take to work through the effects of sexual abuse. I could not control when memories would come. I could not schedule life, and expect supernatural results. I began to live with newfound honesty. I still had more to conquer. I had more to understand about becoming a victor over my abuse. One of the greatest lessons learned—Healing through sexual abuse is a lifelong commitment.

I also learned that wanting to control my healing was another by-product of my sexual abuse. Since I was not in control of my body as a child, I tried to control every aspect of my life.

I even carried that into my sexual relationship with my husband. I got scared to let go. I was afraid that entering a state of sexual abandonment would excavate lost memories. It became a constant challenge to let my guard down as soon as I felt I could not be in control of my reaction to sexual experiences. While I knew consciously God had given us the gift of sex, unconsciously something was crying out to stop. I realized I had to do something about this, beyond praying. I had to make a choice to break the chain of control.

What caused me to need to be in control? What couldn't I let go of? What was just beyond my sights that had power over my life and reactions?

I made the choice to go to a special Saturday appointment with my counselor and ask for her to conduct an EMDR, Eye Movement Desensitization and Reprocessing session with me. When I had first heard of EMDR, which is noted to be an effective way to treat trauma, I was skeptical and scared. I couldn't control my subconscious memory.

Initially, I heard about EMDR in one of our group counseling sessions. One of the other women in our group went through EMDR and uncovered some memories about "Uncle" Michael that she previously did not recall. They literally flashed before her eyes like a film clip that was archived. Afterward, she felt free from the anxious thoughts attached to a memory that had been muted before EMDR. I was supportive of her findings, but this technique was not for me. EMDR freaked me out! I wanted nothing to do with this hocus-pocus. Not to mention, it totally messed with my need to be in control.

The fear of the unknown vanished when I realized I usually dissociated during the sexual violations. Since I felt I could not escape physically, I determined to vanish mentally. Through counseling, I learned these memories were still recorded in my reaction to unrelated incidents. This affected the very part of my marriage that I had tried to preserve over my dating life. I could not allow my anxious thoughts to paralyze me any longer. If I was going to trust God's promise that he would lift me up, I had to "Cast all (my) anxiety on him because he cares for (me)" (I Peter 5:7). I came to the realization that in order to go beyond my numbness, I had to go back to the initial violations. I had to feel what I felt as a little girl, to be able to grieve. As a child I could not afford to feel fear, anxiety, or pain, I had had a greater task—to survive.

I knew that this stronghold of control needed to be broken, and my therapist said I had come to a point where I was ready to deal with some of my dissociation. I was now stable enough to encounter emotionally tough situations. I was told that during EMDR a specific target is identified, in conjunction with a visual image in relationship to negative emotions, followed by an equally powerful, positive belief that can counter it.

In my first session of EMDR, the therapist asked me what issue in my present life I wanted to target. So, I picked the anxiousness brought about by feeling like I was going to lose control during sex. I began to focus on this negative thought. I then focused on an external stimulus;

my therapist's finger moving back and forth. To some extent I felt silly, but was determined to try this method, since it brought healing to my fellow survivor. When my counselor asked me how I felt in these intimate moments, I threw up my guard. I felt immediate vulnerability and anxiousness. In order to deal with my reaction to being out of control, she asked me to visit another situation in life that simulated the same necessity to be in control, but that was less overwhelming.

At the time I was a substitute teacher, mainly in kindergarten. Kids would sometimes surround me, poke me repeatedly, and say, "Teacher! Teacher!" They were just innocently trying to get my attention, but it was a serious trigger point which I could not handle. I would want to shrivel into my skin and take myself away from those instances, take a deep breath, and then ask the children to please back up. But why would unassuming little kindergartners evoke such a severe inner reaction?

Over the next hour, she asked questions concerning my feelings when 30 little fingers were poking my side. She asked about thoughts, feelings, emotions, memories, or sensations that came to me. Nothing. We seemed to go round and round with nothing personally helpful or freeing ... but no magical moments occurred, so maybe this method just was not for me. At one point I said, "This is not working." She encouraged me to stick with her. Within moments, the dam broke loose with a flood of memories. It wasn't the little children's fingers that triggered my emotional response; it was my therapist's finger repeatedly going back and forth. At first, her fingers became Michael's accordion doors shutting behind me. Anxious emotions welled inside me. Tears poured out of my eyes. Then my therapist's fingers became a vile act of sexual abuse. I grabbed tissues to try and clean up. No matter how many tissues I used, I couldn't wipe away the real tears and the subconscious moisture that covered me. Every emotion I could not experience as a child, in order to survive, raged within me. I sat dazed and silent about what had just unfolded ... but in mere moments I realized I sat now consumed by an indescribable peace ... a calm after the storm.

The desensitized little girl in me felt for the first time. As a woman, I brought healing to my wounded little soul by facing the truth.

After discussing the emotional trauma I had just experienced over the past three hours of EMDR, my counselor asked how I felt. Without forethought I said, "I'm alive, so I'm okay."

"Okay?!" My husband was infuriated! "Okay?! You have uncovered the seriousness of your abuse, and you're okay with that?!"

But in my newfound perspective, others have been killed by their abuser. They did not have the chance to rise above it. I was alive and did not have to be re-victimized by hazy memories.

Also, I needed to grieve the premature death of my childhood and its intended purity. It was counterproductive to wallow in my grief. I felt empowered by my newfound freedom.

I knew that there were other areas in my life that needed to be uncovered. That day EMDR was an effective means to be released from one incident of abuse. I understood that different memories would be uncovered at different times of my life. I understood that certain activities and landmarks in life would trigger untapped memories or undesirable feelings.

When I got married, I experienced new challenges related to intimacy. I had to pray for years for Michael to get out of my bedroom. When my daughter turned seven, I wept. I wanted to celebrate her life, but had to dismiss the grief of having my innocence stolen at the age of seven. How could Michael violate someone so beautiful and innocent? Playing Marco Polo with my kids would cause a sense of anxiety to well up in me. The feeling of Michael trying to get his hands all over me in the pool took a while to shake. The more triggers I am able to conquer, the greater freedom I feel. The more I am honest about my fears, the less they own me. The Truth has been at the center of setting me free.

I never realized that the song I grew up singing in Children's Sunday School was a life lesson that would help me through my brokenness, '... The foolish man built his house upon the sand and the house on sand went splat ... The wise man built his house upon The Rock and the house on The Rock stood firm.' [1]

I had built my life on friends, substances, work, and service to others. I had to go back to the basics. I needed to gain understanding about how my worldview was shaped by the mind and actions of a pedophile. I had to realize that my responses were not normal. I wanted to experience greater success and freedom in the process of healing, so I focused on me. I was worth the investment. As I relied on a source greater than myself, The Rock, I would gain sufficient strength to face the skeletons in my protected heart.

CHAPTER FIVE

The Lover

I began to experience a freedom throughout my first year of professional counseling as I faced my past with truth. It was the year leading up to my marriage to my husband, Gary. We wanted to enter marriage with open eyes and insights from a third party. We went to a professional counselor, pastoral counseling (with Doug—of course), and both of us were in group counseling. We were determined to be transparent as we entered a lifelong commitment to one another.

I can hear my transformation in my wedding vows to Gary:

> *The most indescribable thing I have experienced in life is the peace of the Lord. During our time of dating we have experienced many things: joy, sorrow, love, anger, awe, and many other things; and around every incident and emotion I have found a peace from being with you, that peace that surpasses all understanding. I know through Christ's peace that you are the one who He has been preparing for me. In the future, when times are bleak, I vow to remember and re-experience that peace that Christ instilled in my heart, that you are the one He chose for me.*

> *I honor you for taking the time to work through all of the varied hardships that have come our way. I promise to continue this pattern we have started, and even perfect these communication and conflict resolution skills.*

> *In the past two years, and especially the last year, I have discovered the essence of being a true companion of Christ and*

you. This comes from being a seeker of Truth, capital "T," meaning Christ, and small "t," truth and honesty. Our love is stronger than steel, even though some nicks may exist. This armor of steel from the Holy Spirit comes from truth. As it says in Ephesians, "Let us battle life with His armor, His armor of truth, righteousness, peace, faith, salvation, the Holy Spirit and the word of God.

I promise to make Truth the center of our relationship. Either way you write it, Capital 'T'" or small "t," truth is the core of any successful relationship. And against all odds this is what I vow, to be committed to you and our vows, to be three in one 'til death do us part.

Gary spoke truth through his vows:

Martha, I love you. You are so very special to me. You are the one who will make my life complete. You showed me love when I didn't want anybody to love me. When I met you, I didn't want to get married. Now I can't see how I couldn't marry you. Martha, my favorite Bible verse takes on new meaning with you in my life. In John nine, verses three and four, the disciples ask Jesus why this man is blind and Jesus said so that the works of God might be displayed in his life. I loved this verse for many reasons, but as we become one, I pray that the works of God will be displayed through us. Martha, you are a precious gift from God to me. I promise to put your needs before my own. I will love you and be with you through whatever comes our way. From this day on, our family comes second only to God. I will make our home a safe place for all those who enter it. I leave our family in God's hands to do with as He likes. Martha, I know this day seemed like it was never going to get here for us. We are both taking this step after much thought and prayer. I want you to know I take this commitment with great reverence. Te amo.

Throughout my relationship with Gary, I have learned how to love more authentically. At the core of a genuine lover is truth.

I have committed myself to being truthful in life and marriage;

at the same time there are tugs to mask the truth daily. Fine-tuning the differences between truth and concealment of truth is a lifelong challenge, but ultimately, liberation comes from speaking the truth out of love. I needed to relearn how to love and be loved.

At some point, I lost the ability to love myself. When I stood at heights of confidence, I got accused of being a snob. When I lost myself in insecurities, I also got accused of being a snob. Being quiet and withdrawn often is misread as haughtiness, too. (Of course, my sister thinks it's just that I have a turned up nose.)

I needed to learn to love myself and get rid of biting criticisms, quick judgments, and personal assaults. As I worked on loving myself, maybe others could more easily love me for who I was becoming. I knew negative self-talk would eventually snuff out who I wanted to become—and would absolutely make it impossible for me to be loved and be loveable. Self-love would bring about a freedom beyond my fears, enabling me to start the process of healing and living. I knew that as I redefined love, I could better develop a belief that I was worthy of an authentic self-love.

That self-love began with forgiving myself. While I was not guilty of Michael's molestation against me, this seed of perversion led me into poor choices. I had not forgiven myself, even though I had asked God for forgiveness repeatedly. This lack of self-forgiveness kept me in survival mode, not in living victoriously out of a love for myself.

One of my sources of encouragement is music. It repeatedly helps me work through life's challenges. I find empowerment and victory in singing. I am blessed to lead others in worship at church. Countless songs allow me to remember that processing through pain, receiving forgiveness, and finding amazing life through those discoveries bring triumph.

Casting Crowns' song "East to West" touches me each time I sing its lyrics. I find it comforting, that even though I feel as if I've hit an end, forgiveness and second chances are a limitless offer to me. When

I seek forgiveness, my shortcomings are tossed as far as the east is from the west; they are erased from the past. The beauty of this analogy is that north and south hit one of two poles. If you begin walking north or south, eventually you hit a pole and switch directions; you stop walking north and begin walking south. So, if the biblical analogy was that God would throw our sins as far as the south is from the north, He could go to one of the poles and pick up your "stuff," and hurl it right back at you the next time you mess up. But God throws our sins as far as the east is from the west. The east and west have limitless ends. They go on and on, without a stopping point. God hurls our forgiven faults into infinity and beyond. When it comes to our sins, God is a forgetful God. If we admit our faults and ask for forgiveness for them, He is faithful to forgive and forget. Now, that is love!

My Creator's love makes me pure. While I hold onto my failures, He has forgotten them once I admit them and turn away from those poor choices. While I have asked for forgiveness repeatedly for acting out with other children, asking once was enough. I tend to remind God of my faults. I need to stop re-hashing forgiven faults, accept His endless love and forgiveness, and forgive myself.

I needed to seek moments to build myself up with praise, encouragement, and hope. It is awkward, but I have learned a few ways to help.

I don't create mantras that are coined and lose their effectiveness. I grew up hearing enough of those, and quite often, I just tuned them out. When I conquer a fear or a situation, I encourage myself, and thank God for His help. I work on speaking positively about myself to combat the negative messages I let skew the truth throughout my life. I have come to celebrate that I was created for a unique purpose. I once was held captive by negative self-talk, but now I am finding hope in new internal dialogue:

- I am an amazing creation, invaluable to my Creator.

- He loves me so much, that He made me in His image.

- I have been given a spirit of power, love, and self-discipline—not of fear or timidity.

- This pain is momentary. Joy and freedom await me.

- He has amazing plans to bless me, not to harm me.

In loving myself, I'll be a better lover. Love is freeing, not controlling. I am learning to not control every sexual encounter with my husband. The molestation programmed me to fear the unexpected. A man's instinct does not program him to be patient with his sexual drive and desires. My husband has worked on setting aside impulses out of respect for me. Hovering memories, the fear of a memory surfacing, or triggers firing at inopportune times have forced me to ask him to be patient. He has learned patience, because he loves me. His growth in sensing my discomfort has increased my love and appreciation of him. Now my act of love is to strive to set aside the fear of the unknown and truly experience my husband.

Also, with Gary I have to work on receiving praise. I had become conditioned that if people gave me a compliment, they wanted something from me. I would fret about the validity or authenticity of kindness, and not allow a compliment to be accepted. I constantly was on guard. So, I had to learn that not everyone had ulterior motives when speaking encouraging words. And, I continue to remind myself that the burden lays on them if people's compliments are disingenuous. I now strive to hear praise as authentic and unconditional love, and give encouragement out of pure love.

Love is a gift. Authentic and unconditional love is a treasure which is best learned through the example of others. When I was speaking to a group of junior high and high school students, a high school girl approached me in tears, "Please pray for my mom to come and hear you tonight. She needs to hear what you have to say."

That evening I spoke to a small group of parents, and I could tell that the last woman to arrive was the girl's mom. I shared my student presentation to parents. We discussed elements of authentic love and other related topic areas. This mother raised her hand with what I interpreted as being agitation, "What did you teach my daughter?"

With slight hesitation, I responded, "Well, I did not explain any details about my abuse. I just said that a man in church had been inappropriate with me over the period of five years."

"My daughter came home a totally different person. When she was seven years old her mother died, and I became her stepmother. We have never had a relationship, until today ... I loved the relationship we began today, and I don't want that to change back."

Her stepdaughter took the risk to demonstrate true love, not knowing what the response would be. This was a triumphal moment where real, transparent love was reciprocated. It's a risk we all must be willing to try, and try again and again.

As we step out in faith to love and be loved, we may feel we aren't worthy of love. It's truly about you, not about others. If someone fails to see your true worth, it is their loss. You are a creative, valuable individual who does not receive value from the esteem of others. You must start by loving yourself and then taking the risk to love others. You are worthy, now you need to start believing that truth and acting like a valued treasure.

I am valuable and worthy of authentic, unconditional love, in spite of the mixed message Michael implanted in my head. My past, my thoughts, or disillusionment could no longer hold me captive. The plan for my life is freedom. I am worthy of a sweet, empowered, self-disciplined freedom, because I am a conqueror. I must combat the lies that have incarcerated my life and reach out with a hope for the future. As I come to a point of loving myself, I have the potential to create healthier relationships and a healthier life.

One of the greatest acts of self-love I experienced was getting myself into counseling. I entered counseling skeptically and on guard. In the first session, I warned my new therapist, "Don't try any therapeutic games with me. I will just treat them like an acting class exercise; and act my way through them. I want to get to the truth." I needed a professional counselor with whom I could be real, and this woman proved to be a perfect fit for me. As I unveiled the truth to her, I allowed her to love me authentically and unconditionally over time, and this became a milestone in my life.

The greatest attribute to experience and express is love—an unconditional, authentic love.

VICTOR

One who defeats an enemy or opponent.

CHAPTER SIX

The Forgiver

I received my initial apology from "Uncle" Michael surrounded by 2,500 people in the church where I grew up. Our pastor, Chuck Swindoll, stood before his congregation and read the letter penned by Michael. Michael had proved to be masterful at writing thoughtful letters. I received his letters when I was on missions trips abroad. I held my breath with anticipation of what words he would choose to say that he was sorry.

Mere words cannot express the depth of sadness and heartache I feel as I now must tell you all that there have been acts which can only be defined as molestation perpetrated by me in the past upon young girls within this congregation. How I wish I could say, 'It isn't so!' In so doing I have violated these young lives, robbed them of their childhood innocence, and injured them in their normal development to maturity and happiness in ultimate courtship and marriage. And I have violated the trust placed in me by each of their parents. For so doing I have no excuses!

In Matthew 18:6 Jesus states: "Whoever causes one of these little ones who believes in me to stumble, it is better for him that a heavy millstone be hung around his neck, and that he be drowned in the depth of the sea." I feel the weight and condemnation of that millstone about my neck, and know that I am under the chastening rod of the heavenly Father of those precious lives.

This very afternoon I began a sexual addiction counseling program, and pray that God will further open my understanding to the full scope and depth of what I have done—that healing may come to the families I have injured as well as to myself.

I also want you to know the deep sorrow I have over the manner in which I have betrayed your trust in me, and realize that—with such history in my background—I should never have allowed my name to be placed in nomination for eldership. May God forgive me for that incredible error in judgment!

I plead for your prayers as I endeavor to make the remaining years of my life free of such gross hypocrisy, but rather that they will be full of fruitful and consistent living among God's people—as Pastor Chuck has so often said: 'To end well!'

With this statement I submit my resignation from the board of elders of the First Evangelical Free Church of Fullerton.

Dated 9-24-92

But for some reason all I heard were the words that he had thrown around through the investigation and confrontation, "I'm sorry I violated girls' comfort zones with a grandfatherly love." It was just a "grandfatherly exuberance." "I am guilty of having kisses and hugs that seemed to last too long." Michael and Gayle seemed to do everything to justify, minimize, and rationalize his criminal acts against children.

For months I tried to wrap my head around these empty, hurtful words. Counseling did not remove the daggers I felt were plunged in me by those words. And I did not want resentment to destroy me. I wanted to feel a sense of justice. I feared to prosecute him, because I felt I would be laughed off of the witness stand. At that time I only recalled wet kisses. I had no understanding of why my mouth was wet. I wanted the chains of deceit to be broken. I felt that could only happen if I faced my perpetrator and his wife, the accomplice, with the truth as I saw it. They not only had conspired on ways to draw me into their home for insidious purposes, but I now knew that they also plotted on how to trap my niece, who is five years younger than I, into their web of deceit. I could not remain silent any more.

The church arranged a face-to-face meeting. It almost felt like an old Western stand-off. My parents, husband, counselor, Pastor Doug, and myself sat in a straight line. The church counselor and "Uncle" Michael and "Aunt" Gayle sat across from us, just out of reach.

Michael began with a grief-stricken face, "Oh, I miss going to my dear friend's home at ..." (he recited my parents' address). His pathetic plea sent me elsewhere. I couldn't stand the blah blah blah, with no admittance nor transparency. I seemed to fall into a trance of internal questions. Would knowledge give him power over me again? Did I want to give him a window into my soul? Would this be a tantalizing experience for Michael to know he caused me such pain? Hesitancy welled up inside of me before reading my confrontation letter to Michael. I wondered if somehow sharing my thoughts and verbalizing his actions, sucked out all of my power and transferred it to him.

This time to think only amplified my trepidation. The "what ifs" increased my doubt. As I doubted his response, I doubted my ability to face him with the truth. I had to find power from within to speak the truth. I had to discover God's strength as my parents and husband shared their hearts. I knew God didn't bring me this far to be timid. He would give me a spirit of valor. His cry to me was "Fear not, I am with you always. The truth will set you free." If I allowed fear to shackle my authenticity and silence the truth, there was no chance for this experience to set me free. My goal was not to set Michael free; he would have to take that up all on his own.

Somehow, I snapped out of my trance when it was my turn to share my scripted confrontation. I remained composed and stuck to the words I had written for a dramatic impact to my captive audience, Michael and Gayle. After I finished, I looked up, with no apparent effect on Michael and Gayle. My counselor gently laid her hand on my arm, and said, "That was very articulate, but now can you just speak from your heart about how Michael's actions affected you?"

I took a deep breath and let Michael and Gayle into my world even more. I remember speaking about a specific sexual incident; Michael's wife, Gayle jumped in quickly, "How could you say such a thing!?"

Michael remained silent.

"Gayle, you were in the house every time I was there, but you conveniently disappeared each time the abuse took place. Where were you?"

With a nasally, matter-of-fact response, she said, "Well, I can show you my calendar."

All of us sat stone silent. What did that mean? Was this just another coping mechanism? Did she stick her head in her calendar of events, and write, "I am making lunch for Michael and Martha while they are 'playing' "? What kind of twisted response was that?

At one point, I looked Michael in the eyes and said, "I forgive you."

"Thank you! Thank you! You forgive me!" he exhaled. He spoke these words in one breath, as if he had held his breath with pent-up anticipation for this moment, to be let free.

"Wait! Obviously you do not understand the true meaning of forgiveness." I went on educating him on my newfound meaning of forgiveness.

"Forgiving you means I am no longer shackled to you. I release you. You are no longer my problem or my burden. It is between you and God. God was in the room every time. You can't hide the truth from Him. He was there. You can choose to deal with it on earth, or wait until you are face to face with your Maker. You will not be able to lie to Him. He knows the truth. He was there."

It felt so good to pass the baton. I decided to live above his degradation and chose to not let his actions and attitudes shape my own. My heart transformed that day.

I released him to his Maker, who was present when he abused me.

He could choose to work out his trespasses on children with fear and trembling on earth, or wait until it was too late. That would be even a more fearful situation, than facing it all right then and there. He *will* be held accountable for his actions against children. Thankfully, this was no longer on my shoulders. "I release you. You are no longer my burden to bear."

I don't worry about encountering Michael in heaven. My perspective has become "Father knows best." Who am I to know if Michael has worked out his "stuff" with God? I have enough of my own "stuff" to work through, that I don't need to take on the weight of Michael's crimes. When I forgave him, I could not second-guess the response, or the lack of reaction I got from Michael and Gayle. I felt sorry for both of them. What a weight to haul.

I envisioned the shackles Ebenezer Scrooge potentially would drudge through eternity, if he did not look back on his life and how he could transform his future. I came to Michael and Gayle, like Scrooge's former business partner, Jacob Marley. I came with my shackles. Fortunately, unlike Marley, my end had not come, and I had started to face how I had been bound to my abuse and abuser. I did not have to be in heavy chains, as punishment for my sinful responses to my abuse. I had a message to give Michael and Gayle; they could be free through facing the truth about their character. Scrooge took the bait and transformed his life on earth, before it was too late. Michael and Gayle have been warned that they need an Ebenezer Scrooge moment, if they do not want to suffer the consequences of their lifestyle of lies and deceit for an eternity. But that was not my load to carry.

I have realized through the process of forgiveness that pedophiles and their spouses usually cannot apologize in a manner that will be sufficient. Most survivors who have sought apologies from their perpetrator have shared experiences. Their perpetrators apologized without a detailed explanation of what they did wrong. When confronted with specific instances of abuse, they seem to play dumb. They quite often believe our memories are exaggerated. They may admit some indiscretions, but rarely come clean about the laundry list of soiled truths. Even those who mean to be sincere at heart, seem to fail.

Perpetrators are unable to understand the rawness of our emotions, because they have lived a masked identity. They have not tapped into their emotional beings at all. Their feelings may be real, but if they were truly to seek understanding, they would crumble under the weight of their wickedness. It would be like an old cartoon where the character tried to plug a reservoir's crack with a finger, and then another crack burst, and then another, and another ... the character did not have enough appendages to block the outpour of water, nor would the exposed, transparent pedophile. The dam would burst uncontrollably. Perpetrators have so much brokenness plaguing their lives that they feel they cannot risk opening up the floodgates.

Victims have the right to question pedophiles about the sexual offenses perpetrated against them. However, I believe that when perpetrators discount their victims' memories, they are not being arrogant, nor are they in denial. They really do not remember; they cannot afford to. If they were to playback the filmstrip of their life as an abuser, it would destroy them. Each account has been filed "Top Secret." If I, as a victim of sexual abuse, dissociated from my abuse, is it not possible that Michael did the same with his acts of abuse? Dissociation is an amazing coping mechanism, where I found years of solace. I later discovered that Michael's aunt victimized him at the age of ten. So, it is probable that he mastered dissociation at a young age, and used it throughout his adult life as a predator of sexual abuse. His mind has protected him to the point that the weight of his offenses has virtually disappeared, so that he can live.

As I let go of Michael through forgiveness that day, I recognized that he was blinded by a self-serving, sexual addiction. My anger and disgust turned into grief for him, his hardened heart, and his depraved mindset. With this shift it became easier to let go, and release the ties that bound me to Michael for so long. It no longer mattered how Michael responded that day. I needed to realize that forgiveness was about the position of my heart. Michael was the only one who could search his heart and be accountable for his actions.

The ultimate act of release brings contentment as we allow the Righteous Judge, God, to be in control of vengeance and grace. I don't want to live life stressing about Michael's repentance, because truly, I would not know the state of his heart. God knows the depths of his thoughts and the authenticity of his words. Holding onto him is a waste of my time and effort. I am not qualified to get even, so I release him.

Pastor Doug said, "This reminds me of a section in Romans, 'Do not repay anyone evil for evil. Be careful to do what is right in the eyes of everybody. If it is possible, as far as it depends on you, live at peace with everyone. Do not take revenge, my friends, but leave room for God's wrath...' " (Romans 12:17-19).

I love the last line, "Leave room for God's wrath." If I seek to settle the score, I just won't do it as well as God. My job is to forgive, not to avenge. So, I choose to forgive and let God deal with Michael and Gayle's lack of repentance.

I realize that not all victims of sexual abuse will have the opportunity for face-to-face forgiveness due to death, unwillingness, or distance. Do not falsely believe this means you will be shackled to your past your whole life. Forgiveness is a state of the heart. Forgiveness is being free from bitterness. Forgiveness is a process of letting go, and putting it at the feet of the Righteous Judge. Forgiveness releases resentment from controlling you. Forgiveness allows you not to be defined by your discontent. Forgiveness is about freeing you. Forgiveness opens up the door for peace and true joy.

Forgiveness becomes the launching point as we release our perpetrators into their Creator's hands. I know when memories of my abuse or moments directly affected by my abuse pop up, I have to choose to forgive the murder of my childhood innocence. I will not allow resentment to fester or grow. I choose to let God take care of vengeance. By releasing my abuser to the TRUE JUDGE, I am free.

Forgiveness seeks a miracle. As we strive to forgive, we hope for something beyond ourselves. We ask ourselves to love the fallible person, who acted out of selfish depravity. We continue to hate what they did, but seek to discover forgiveness beyond those acts. Out of love for ourselves, we set our prison mates free. We are on a path to healing beyond the shackles slapped on by our memories. We need to allow the Judicator to bring justice.

At six-months-old, I won
a Beautiful Baby Contest.
People continued to
comment on my spunky
personality and ability to
follow directions.

The Christmas card photo for
1969. My sister, Ruth, was fifteen
when I was born.

Curiosity and fun
filled my life in my
early years. People
continuously stopped
my parents, asking if I
was in commercials.

Setting my hair in
curlers became a daily
task. The natural curl
didn't happen until I
got a perm in 1985. It
brought on a whole new
meaning of the word
"perm."

Before I began
acting I could hang
out at my childhood
home. However,
once I began
working, I was
rarely in Orange
County.

I stayed home from school one day to learn to ride a bike for a commercial audition. In the interview, I only had to stand next to the bike, not ride it.

When I lost teeth or my teeth were cutting through I would get high fevers. The night before my final audition for the second Mickey Mouse Club, I lost a tooth. I barely pulled through the singing and dancing, but my fever sapped my energy and I did not land the role.

For many of my composite photos for acting, I would go to "Uncle" Michael's house. He had a kid-friendly environment. If you look closely at the left-hand photo, you will see his hand in the bottom right-hand corner. In the photo with the glasses, he is playing Chinese checkers with me.

My niece, Heather, lived in Nebraska in her early childhood. When she moved back to California, she, too, became a victim of "Uncle" Michael.

As I started to develop, I began to create ways to escape the perpetual sexual abuse at "Uncle" Michael and "Aunt" Gayle's house.

The Waltons welcomed me into their family in 1979. Kami Cotler (Elizabeth) acted like a big sister during the year I played Serena.

Judy Norton Taylor (Mary Ellen) and I played on *The Waltons* weekend softball team against other television cast and crew teams.

I poured myself into charity events. Alison Arngrim (Nellie on *Little House on the Prairie*) and I frequented many. Little did we know that each of us were experiencing the effects of sexual abuse. Currently, Alison is on the National Advisory Board of The National Association to Protect Children (www.PROTECT.org), fighting to give children a legal and political voice in the war against child abuse.

I felt honored to win Homecoming Queen in 1984. Months later, during Christmas vacation, I landed a role on a cable sit-com, and finished my senior year on the set.

My *Walton* castmates: Keith Coogan (Jeffrey), Lisa Harrison (Toni), and Jon Walmsley (Jason) surprised me at my eighteenth birthday. I had no idea the joy surrounding my birthday would be snuffed out a couple of days later when I was fired from the cable sit-com. It felt like my world fell apart.

After a year of facing my perpetrator and the truths surrounding the effects of my sexual abuse, Gary and I entered marriage with open minds and dedicated hearts. We committed ourselves to one another on September 18, 1993, surrounded by family and friends.

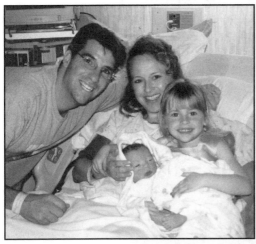

Preparing for the birth of my children became a challenge that I had to leave in God's hands. I worked through my gripping fears of not being able to be in control and experiencing pain during the delivery by journaling Scripture and songs to carry me through the birthing process. Being completely reliant on His strength proved to be quite liberating.

My parents and husband enjoyed watching Ryder (Ishmaelite), Bailey (Children's Chorus), and I (Narrator) perform in the musical, *Joseph and the Amazing Technicolor Dreamcoat.*

In Indonesia, I went to schools and orphanages to speak about each child's personal value. I passed out gold-covered chocolates to emphasize this message of hope.

In my mission to stop childhood sexual abuse, I have been to Southern Brazil. We made sword balloons as a reminder to fight lies and secrets with the truth.

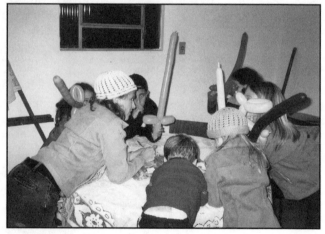

As the founder of *A Quarter Blue*, I have been asked to train various law enforcement groups. My personal experience brings insights beyond academies' training.

CHAPTER SEVEN

The Justice Seeker

"Hello, this is Detective Joe Romo." The officer told me that an investigation was underway. A victim had heard the re-broadcast of the sermon when Michael was excommunicated. She wondered if he had served time for his crime. Unable to build the case around her story, the police were searching for other victims' testimonies. Ten years prior, I was fearful of trial, and wanted to focus on my healing. At this moment, though, I felt more empowered, and realized I might be able to keep Michael from molesting other little girls.

I named the women in our group, the girls I believed were victims who never received help, and my niece. Over the time of their investigation they chose to build the case around my niece. Her memories were detailed. She also hadn't participated in our group therapy at church. Due to the fact that Michael was a creature of habit, it could appear that we were adapting our testimonies to be identical. Over the course of a year there were many hearings. My mom, husband, and various church leaders were faithful to attend. I wanted to remain detached as they went back and forth with technicalities. I wanted to guard my heart and not jump on this uncertain roller coaster ride. I really didn't want to be in the same room with Michael and Gayle, until I knew consequences for his actions had been determined.

Michael was given a plea agreement if he pled guilty. He would receive a sex offender card and be on probation for seven years. While it seemed like a minor sentence for all the sexual counts against Michael, it was better than no accountability at all. Now I was ready to face him in court.

My niece and I were dressed in outfits stylish and enviable. We wanted Michael to see he hadn't robbed us of class and confidence. We would face Michael's wife and sister, and Michael in front of a judge. It was sentencing day. We were going to tell our story. We were armed with our letters, ready to stand strong in front of a crowded room and speak the truth about Michael. Mine read:

Part of me doesn't even want to share with you the way you impacted my life, because somehow I think in your sick, perverse mind you will find pleasure in it. Both Heather and I thought of bringing a picture of us at the ages in which the abuse started. I thought of bringing a picture of my daughter, since she is the age I was when I met you, but I do not want you to even have the opportunity to lust after who Heather and I were, and who my beautiful, innocent daughter is and will remain. If there is any good out of what you did (and I give you absolutely no credit for what God is doing through a Heaven-sent husband and ongoing counseling), I am learning how to protect my daughter and son from criminals like you.

I am thankful that earthly justice has been pursued concerning your sexual violations against children. While I am grateful Heather has her day in court, today, I am frustrated that your lewd and ungodly acts against me will not be tried in open court. However, I must rely on more than man-made laws, because they will always fall short and know that no matter how you were sentenced it would not equate or diminish the life sentence you gave me.

You are guilty of much more than sexual immorality.

You are guilty of lying for you claimed and still claim to be a Christian, the problem with this is you are representing who Christ is and have repeatedly misrepresented who He is, for He said, 'But if anyone causes one of these little ones who believe in me to sin, it would be better for him to have a millstone hung around his neck and to be drowned in the depths of the sea.' The judge saved you from the torture that would have been inflicted upon you by prisoners. Because he knows that even murderers consider you the lowest of the low. They detest and inflict punishment upon child molesters in jail, so how much more will God hold you accountable for your repulsive sexual acts against children? I have to question if that is why you have beat prostate cancer and continue to live, because you fear that death will bring you face-to-face with your Creator, who is there when you weasel your way into numerous families and sexually violate their daughters and granddaughters, while you pose as a trustworthy member of the Christian community.

You are guilty of murder—for you murdered my purity and childhood innocence.

You are guilty of lying—for you lied about your innocence.

You are guilty of deceit—for you continue to deceive your friends and family members who even stand by your side today.

You are guilty of trespassing—for you trespass into the bedroom I share with my husband and paralyze sexual intimacy in a God-centered marriage.

You are guilty of destroying families, inflicting sexual promiscuity, and abusing your power and access to countless children including missionary children and children overseas ... this list of your guilt goes on and on and is rooted in evil, malice, slander, heartlessness, and arrogance ... but your greatest charge will be that you turned children from Christ ... Michael, you will face serious judgment beyond today's sentencing. You may have people who are standing beside you; and I feel so sorry that they are trapped in your unending lie. They need to ask themselves first how could so many women of such a wide age span and walks of life all have the same story. Secondly, what did each of us have to gain by bringing this to the police ... do you think we really want to relive that and be stuck in this deceitful game you have played with the courts and our emotions?! The truth is you are a pedophile, who abused the trust of parents and children, and stole way more than you could ever repay because of your sexual sins and exploitations. You are free technically as you walk out that door today, with some imposed restrictions by the court, and the only reason I consider myself free is because I have a Savior in Jesus ... what about those victims of yours who turned away from Jesus ... woe to you who caused more than one of these little ones who believed in Jesus to sin, remember ... 'it would be better for (you) to have a millstone hung around (your) neck and to be drowned in the depths of the sea.' My solace is in that your eternal sentencing will come another day.

I held the paper in my hand, ready to face my perpetrator once again with the truth. This time felt different. I was more comfortable in my own skin. I was grateful that finally he would serve some earthly justice, and not be able to diminish the truth with a deceptive presence. I briefly caught a glimpse of him. He seemed deflated and aged. It made me feel sorry for him; the burden of lies and deceit seemed to have finally weighed heavily on him. With a handful of family members and leadership from the church, we waited, thankful that the sentencing had arrived. The assistant district attorney ran out with an expression of jubilee, "You will never believe what happened. The judge re-read the evidence and he said that if he sentenced Michael today, he would go to prison for seven years." Because of the severity of the abuse, the plea agreement had been rejected by the judge, and the case would go to trial.

So, we were seemingly back to square one. The process would start over. My heart, spilled on the pages of my victim impact statement, would have to wait to be heard. I felt a sense of relief that the judge saw through the masquerade. I was hopeful that earthly justice would prevail. These hopes were dashed. Before Michael would see his day in court, he was released from any wrongdoing—the California Supreme Court altered the statute of limitations. We were no longer allowed to press charges for the abuse that occurred during our childhood. It was deemed unconstitutional. Countless perpetrators were released, including mine.

Michael was never convicted, and neither was Gayle for aiding in these crimes against children. They live in a retirement complex in San Diego, California.

It seems like most of us who were victimized by Michael were not ready to tell our stories to the authorities until it was too late.

I already understood that I had to rely on more than man-made laws, because they will always fall short. However, my desire is a day will arrive when lawmakers and enforcers will see and understand the heart of child molestation.

I have to find contentment that Michael's true sentencing will come another day. The legal system can only attempt to bring justice to child molesters, for true justice is on the other side.

CHAPTER EIGHT

The Truth Hunter

While being intimate with my husband, I was on the brink of a memory. I had to force myself to stay present with him, and not slip into my old ways of dissociation. This peculiar sensation made me feel like a prop, not the woman whom my husband treasured. I knew in my head that my husband had no intention of hurting me, but I couldn't shake the sense that nails were shrieking down the face of a chalkboard. In my heart, I really did not want to remember, but I wanted to know if I had formed these feelings out of fear. Later on in the day, I made a phone call to my niece. I simply asked if I should sense something eerily familiar about a certain type of touch. She simply replied, "Yes."

My niece and I stored our memories very differently. Most of my life, I remembered very little of the actual inappropriate acts of Michael. I had stored reactions and symptoms of the sexual abuse, but very little concrete memories about the molestation. My niece, on the other hand, has vivid memories of Michael's sexual acts and his jaded reprimanding when she shared her disgust and discomfort. We have not shared the details of our own abuse with one another. I do not want to take on her memories and make them mine. It is possible that our stories are different; however, every point we have discussed has been identical. Some victims are like my niece, haunted by unforgettable memories and descriptive dreams. Others of us live in a hollow tunnel of shadows and whispers of hints of what took place behind closed doors. Both are valid. The person with minimal memories does not need to feel that their trauma is somehow minimized.

While as victims of sexual abuse, we may not remember all of the details of our exploitation; this does not mean we are avoiding the truth. It is difficult to understand why some victims have very vivid memories of their abuse, and why others have a multitude of the effects, but very scattered memories of the actual sinister acts.

I escaped memory recall through dissociation. I counted white slats on the window blinds on every window. I learned the Portuguese language on the sign over his head. I gazed into the black and white photos of Michael and Gayle when they served as pilot and nurse in World War II. I got lost in the texture of the white, chenille bedspread. I became a master of disappearing into the elements of the room, and discovering the uniquenesses of them. So, my memories of the actual abuse are minimal. I found myself lost in another world.

I do not believe this is a form of denial or repression. I am confident this was a protective shield unintentionally donned. I wish, as a child, that I had felt empowered to stop the abuse, but since I felt defenseless by the fear of disobedience, instead of fighting, I retreated.

Some people might find fault in this brief defense of memory retrieval therapies, especially in light of the possibility of created memories and false allegations. This is not the place I want to banter back and forth about repressed memories and false allegations. I am not an expert in the field; I am a participant within it. I want to encourage all survivors to only seek professional help in memory retrieval, if there is something that needs to be unlocked to further the healing process. I believe not all of us are meant to remember everything. I encourage people to not approach memory retrieval with a "bring it on" attitude. Beauty does not come out of rushing through anything, for rushing breeds confusion and chaos. Taking on all points of brokenness at once may cause a domino effect. You may find yourself not being able to stop the collapse, as you realize how many facets of your life were affected by your past abuse.

Most memories will fall before you when it is time. I believe when the Bible says that God will only give you as much as you can handle, that means you will only be given memories that you can manage at the very time you remember.

We each need to ask ourselves if we will become healthier, if we remember specific details. For those of us who have limited recollection, we need not feel like we must have more concrete evidence of a cause for our dysfunction. Sexual abuse does not have to be detailed to be traumatic.

I feel for people when they tell me, "My perpetrator was just my uncle, at least it wasn't my father." Or "He just touched me, at least he didn't ...." "Just" is a word that should have no place when addressing sexual abuse. Teens or adults misusing their power and strength for sexual gratification with children is wrong, and will not leave victims unharmed or indifferent.

In my first year of therapy, I felt the need to address my inability to not be in control. Chapter four shared my experience with EMDR, Eye Movement Desensitization and Reprocessing. This treatment allowed me to play back the film of a certain sexual experience that started to cripple sexual relations with my husband. Under treatment that day, I processed through my deep-seated emotions and was able to become desensitized to that memory.

I believe professional memory recall should be sought only for personal growth. Reaching back in time in order to press charges against a perpetrator with newfound, concrete memories is dangerous.

EMDR allows me to discuss my abuse with freedom from guilt or shame. At the same time, it also would have made me an ineffective witness for testimony in a trial. Jurors want to see victims gripped by their abuse, or they deduce it did not really happen. EMDR walked me through the trauma to a point of peace.

We must find contentment in facing one point at a time. We may not need to remember every offense perpetrated against us. The memory of sexual abuse is enough. Remembering each grievous act will not change how we attack the effects of sexual abuse. We need not underestimate our need for healing if we are unable to remember the details of abuse. Our consciences store memories that we respond to through impulses, even though we are without certain concrete memories.

I have chosen to look upward when I am overwhelmed. One song that has become a life song for me is MercyMe's "Bring the Rain." I cry out for joy, peace, and freedom in the midst of the memories. I search for ways to praise Him for allowing me to experience certain traumas so that true character and beauty break forth. I have no doubt that I truly need a perfect shelter in the storm. In knowing Him, it's safer to discover myself.

I have learned more about me than I ever remembered before— thanks to a social networking site and speaking opportunities. As discussed previously, I discovered that I was the initiator of sexual abuse after giving a Croatian interview. I also received a friend request from a name I didn't recognize. The woman wrote:

> I am not sure whether you'll remember me. My family was very good friends with Michael and Gayle (it wasn't until high school that I found out that we weren't really related to them, as they were always Aunt Gayle and Uncle Michael to us) and I remember playing with you on many occasions at their home. I think we may have been at church together as well. I am about nine months older than you. I never forgot about you and wondered many times what became of you. And, I just found you here. I then did a Google search and discovered your Website for your non-profit organization and everything came together. I am so very sorry to hear that you suffered from Michael's terrible actions. That breaks my heart. My sister was mistreated by him but somehow I escaped notice. Though, I did endure abuse of many forms in my own home and ultimately ended up in a foster home for several years.
>
> Since then, though, life has been much kinder to me and I am doing well. With the help of a tenacious spirit, good therapy, and some distance from California, I have recovered well. I, too, have turned my energies toward helping others heal from their wounds of

many kinds. I work as a psychotherapist now as part of my career ménage.

I have one particular distinct memory of you as a child when I sensed that you were afraid and upset, and I can't help but wonder now how that fits into this bigger picture. You were in a camper and I joined you for a short ride, perhaps to church. You didn't say much and I remember wondering what was wrong. I also have a memory of showing you how to play a game that they had with a little metal marble that traveled through a labyrinth. We were so young and it was so long ago, but for some reason, I've never forgotten those things.

A number of years ago, I found out about Michael's abusive actions. It was after the fact, as I have not lived in CA for many years. I was completely heartbroken and felt so betrayed. I talked to someone at EV Free about it to get more information and they were great about telling me everything I wanted to know. I ultimately wrote Michael and Gayle a letter, basically asking why he didn't get help, why she didn't do something, and how he could have done such a thing. Their response was to invite me, at their expense, to come to visit them and to sit down with them and their counselor to talk about it. I appreciated the gesture and contemplated taking them up on it, but I was so afraid that he would try to make excuses or to displace the blame and so I couldn't do it. I wanted to find out what was going on inside his head, but I didn't know if I could handle it. They still send me Christmas cards and it's a difficult thing for me—so complicated.

This is a very long note and I hope you don't mind the contact. It was just important to me to let you know that you are thought of fondly, to express my sadness over reading about your own history with them, and to wish you well in your own healing and in your wonderful work with others. Blessings.

Her mention of the camper made me realize something. My recall of cold French fries was authenticated. I had encountered abuse in the camper bed! Michael would order the French fries from the driver's seat, then come into the camper shell after parking in the fast food chain's parking lot. The French fries were cold because I had to earn my reward through sexual acts before being allowed to eat them.

Another childhood friend found me through a social networking site. I had never told her about my abuse, but after she read my story on-line, she recalled a Christmas spent at my home. "Oh, my gosh! That must have been him. This man came over and you grabbed me by the hand and tried to rush me upstairs. You told me that he gave you the creeps. But your dad scolded you for being rude to your visitors. You were instructed to come downstairs immediately. I had never seen you act so defiantly to your father, but you did not want to be around that man. Martha, you were trying to protect me."

A sense of relief came over me. I was not always the predator. I tried to save a friend from experiencing the same hellacious experiences I did.

In my mind's eye, God has a jar where He stores all our lost memories. (For me, as a survivor of sexual abuse, there are MANY!) He holds onto them until we are ready for a morsel of our past. We can work through our pasts without knowing every detail. We should not focus our healing efforts on our memories of sexual abuse. We need to focus on the effects.

Some of you are overwhelmed with memories of atrocities never told. You long for a sleep-filled night, with dreams and not recurring nightmares. While I do not have personal experience in breaking through repressed memories, I would like you to try to find a counselor with whom you feel safe. Start telling your story. Take those nightmares trapped in your head out of your head and into the counselor's lap. The longer those memories and thoughts are imprisoned in your mind, the more empowerment you give your past.

Focus on what you can learn from those memories. Vow to never coax a child into a sexual relationship. Determine to love authentically and unconditionally. Establish new guidelines to protect yourself, without boxing out the world or over-controlling each circumstance. Shift the unhealthy, unbalanced patterns you have established in your life.

The key to unlocking freedom is not memories. We must stretch toward what lies ahead, not strain to regain the past.

The animated film *The Incredibles* illustrates this comcept in a thought-provoking manner. The family tried to go underground in suburbia America after mounting lawsuits forced the government to put them in a witness protection program. They masked themselves in urban wear and attempted to melt into society. But they couldn't deny their true gifts and identities, and ultimately they realized that society needed them. They could have cowered in fear about the threat of lawsuits, but they regained a healthy perspective. The memories of the past can paralyze you, too, into a mundane, anonymous life. Or, like Elastigirl, you can realize the person you were created to be and stretch toward your incredible, victorious future.

CHAPTER NINE

The Woman of Process

As Michael drew me in between his legs, I cringed at the thought of being pulled up to his crotch ... AGAIN. I first looked at the familiar sign, "Lar Doce Lar," "Home Sweet Home." I inhaled a breath of endurance, wondering how long I would have to disappear into nothingness. A strange sense fell over me. It seemed as if over Michael's left shoulder, I saw the face of Jesus weeping.

Sometimes, I wonder if this memory was merely something I made up to understand His sorrow over the ongoing abuse, but the vision remains clear. When I studied the Bible, I found myself loving the verse, "Jesus wept" (John 11:35). If God incarnate shed tears as He faced the death of his friend, Lazarus, He must weep every time a child dies inside at the hand of a pedophile.

When I have been asked if I resent God because of my abuse, I honestly answer, "No." I think many people feel I must be living in denial if I am not pointing my finger at God. How could God turn His head to such a horrible crime against children?

I do not see that God's hand was in the center of this confusing relationship at all, or that He turned His head away in apathy. I saw Him look me straight in the eye and speak volumes through His tears.

God grieved that a man would use His name to proclaim Christ with his mouth, but use that same mouth for such evil and perverse acts. Michael would help many people in need with his hands, while using those same hands to violate countless little girls. Michael was not of God.

Michael used a seemingly full-proof front to fool many and deface the character of God.

However, such confusion and duplicity is NOT of God. He is unable to be confusing; it is counter to His personality. If God is truth and light like He proclaims, His hand was not in the dark and deceitful ways of my perpetrator.

I see life as a battle between good and evil. That evil is constantly vying for our attention. Satan's primary desire is to confuse and blind us to the fact that God loves us. Satan is the father of all lies. If this tension did not exist, there would not be a felt need for God.

If God is love, and that love is unconditional, He detests the opposite. Pedophilia is a conditional love. Typically, when children withdraw from their perpetrator, they are punished, threatened, or put down. God does not withdraw from us. He says that He will never leave us or forsake us, so it is not He who withdrew.

Evil is an ongoing theme in this world. One day, I tried to determine how I could withstand the ongoing battle. I realized I had a good example to follow. Jesus withstood torturous beatings, even though He was innocent. I was able to recognize that I, too, withstood severe pain, even though I was innocent. I was in good company. I combed through the pages of the account of the crucifixion wondering how He did it. It hit me! He lived above His circumstances. While He felt every physical and verbal blow, He took a step back from the heinous beatings. He acknowledged His death had a purpose. His death would give life for those who believed in His purpose, to give abundant life beyond their pain and suffering on earth. I had a choice to live above the unfair treatment I endured. Or I could hold on tightly, suffocating under the weight of the seemingly unforgiveable. Could I find purpose in my abuse?

Through this insight, I discovered that, repeatedly, my abuse has been used for the good of others. Out of my life experience, I have been able to educate parents and teachers how to better protect children from sexual abuse. I have been given opportunities to train up numerous professionals and parents how to recognize characteristics and ploys of pedophiles and the signs of sexual abuse. I have been privileged to encourage survivors of sexual abuse that they are not alone in how they think and in the healing process. I have been able to speak worth into many people giving them hope to persevere. The treasures I have been given because of my experiences now far outweigh the pain I endured physically and emotionally during my early life.

"In this you rejoice, though now for a little while, if necessary, you have been grieved by various trials, so that the tested genuineness of your faith—more precious than gold that perishes though it is tested by fire" (1 Peter 1:6-7 ESV).

The phrase "if necessary" stopped me dead in my tracks. I grabbed a pen and underlined it. The only reason I had suffered is because it was necessary to develop my faith. I rose out of the rubble triumphantly! Like gold! Victoriously, I burst through the fire that sought to scorch and destroy me.

In preparing for a trip to speak in Brazil about breaking through the fires in life so that a radiant beauty may be revealed, I found an analogy that I couldn't wait to share. A woman comes across a Bible verse and wants to truly understand the biblical reference about people being refined and purified like silver.

She went accordingly, and without telling him the reason for her visit, begged the silversmith to tell her about the process of refining silver. After he had fully described it to her, she asked, "Sir, do you sit while the work of refining is going on?"

"Oh, yes ma'am," replied the silversmith; "I must sit and watch the furnace constantly, for, if the time necessary for refining is exceeded in the slightest degree, the silver will be injured."

The lady at once saw the beauty and comfort of the expression, "He shall sit as a refiner and purifier of silver."

God sees it necessary to put His children into the furnace; but

His eye is steadily intent on the work of purifying, and His wisdom and love are both engaged in the best manner for us. Our trials do not come at random, and He will not let us be tested beyond what we can endure.

Before she left, the lady asked one final question, "How do you know when the process is complete?"

"That's quite simple," replied the silversmith. "When I can see my own image in the silver, the refining process is finished." [2]

I am in a refining process, a heated, sometimes daunting process. Countless people encounter hardships. It is what I do with those challenges that would make me a Vic"thor" or a Vic"dumb." As a Vic"thor," I could become one who rises victoriously, like the noted Norse god of thunder from mythology, who fought off the forces of evil. Or I could be a Vic"DUMB!" I have a choice. In the face of adversity, I must decide if I want to be a victor or victim. I daily need to determine if I will conquer my personal challenges, for my attitude and perspective will affect the outcome. I also need to surround myself with people who believe in my process and me as an individual. Who I choose to surround myself with shapes my self-perception, my healing process, and my destiny.

I am constantly striving to strike the balance between humility and tenacity as I strive to rise up victoriously. I must have the humility to seek help beyond myself when I need a new perspective. I live in a relentless battle—developing the tenacity to fight through the fear and shame, as an open victor over molestation.

I appreciate the candor of a survivor who has become my friend. As she read and edited my book, she shot off an email to me, fearful that I would not respect her suggestions, because of her place on the path of healing:

Martha, I appreciate that you would be willing to add bits of my story to your book. I've done a lot of thinking about it, and I just don't know what I could add that would be helpful. I do not think about my abuse often, but that is because I spend most of my time avoiding it. What I remember is too much and what I cannot remember scares me. And I have nightmares like crazy!!!

I was reading today (while editing) about the Rapid Eye Movement therapy, and I was not sure whether to feel hopeful or sick to my stomach at the idea of remembering what my mind has worked so hard to forget.

My story is really not a hopeful one ... and I do NOT say that as a victim. I simply say that as one who is crawling and clawing through life as best and as numb as possible. There are some things that are so bad that there should never be any speaking of them again. Know what I mean?

And I am NOT holding onto my pain as some sort of trophy, either. It drives me nuts when people do that!!!

However, I learned after my first and most horrible suicide attempt that I was neither brave enough to die, nor brave enough to live. So now I make it through my days the best that I can. I have a lot of scars, outside and inside. I do the best I can with my marriage, even though my sexuality is my best friend and my worst enemy. I hold onto whatever anesthesia possible, and after losing my Dad, I sleep way too much of my days away.

I am committed to your project and to your mission. I love the LORD. I love my Bible. But I am not very good at being open and honest and raw ... there are secrets that I'm afraid might tear my world apart. And there are impulses that could ruin me.

My heart's desire is not to tout my victories to diminish your current pain and fears. Each of our paths will be different and feel unique. For me, I have found the more I talk about my life and the knowledge I have acquired about prevention and healing, the more liberated I have become about my past. It is a constant letting go.

I discovered this principle in talking to a friend following her husband's suicide. She was left with three children to raise on her own, and had spent her life dedicated to caring for her husband and children. One day we were talking on the phone about how she was coping through life's new challenges. She typically felt relief laying her burdens at the feet of Jesus. She held onto some guilt for feeling overwhelmed by the burden of responsibility and weight of her heavy, longing heart. I asked her, "Sue, don't you think that letting go is an ongoing process? You will constantly be faced with memories of Stewart ... when you give your daughter away after you have walked her down the aisle. Don't you think healing is an ongoing process? A constant letting go, a constant releasing?"

She agreed. "I don't think anyone should expect you to get over the loss of your husband once and for all."

Healing is a process. There is no quick fix or an instant vanishing act for memories of sexual abuse. I walk with millions of former victims of sexual abuse. We are on a path of wholeness as we reach forward into our hopeful futures and diminishing pasts.

BRAT

Main Entry: brat

1 it's not what you think

2 Boldly Resolving Abuse Together

CHAPTER TEN

The BRAT

"What the *@%! happened to you?!" asked a fellow actor whom I adored as a child on *Days of Our Lives*.

I began to matter-of-factly share the story I have told for the past six years.

"You are wearing the most impenetrable shield I have ever seen ..."

I tried to defend my lack of emotion attached to the facts of my abuse, "I tell my story so often, I am not gripped by the truth of the abuse."

"You obviously have not dealt with your abuse ... You have the lowest self-esteem ..." He tried to lessen the blow, "I realize I am projecting my life. I was also molested ..."

The insults and accusations continued, "You should hate your parents ... You hate your child for not stopping the abuse ... You will never forgive her for not standing up to your perpetrator."

"I don't think I hate my child, but I will continue to search myself for the truth. I am about following the truth ... I'll make an appointment with my counselor to find out her insights. The Truth is the center of who I am."

"You haven't even scraped the truth. That's why your organization isn't growing."

The ongoing onslaught of insults kept hurling toward me for at least four hours. On the two-hour drive home, I felt physically ill. Were there truths amongst the offenses thrown at me? I couldn't get home fast enough to make an appointment with my therapist.

"Am I in denial? Or did he misinterpret the peace I have in Christ? Is it because I tell my story so much? Is it because of the EMDR?"

In one word, one of the people who knows me best, my counselor, answered, "Yes."

Sometimes we are so into our abuse, and how it negatively affects our lives, that we cannot get out of the despair and rubble and see beyond the pain. We hold on so tightly, and want everyone to say exactly what we've dreamed—thinking it will make everything better. I have learned that true maturity and release comes from understanding people are unique, and nothing anyone says will magically erase our past. Did I dream of my parents saying sorry as soon as they found out about my abuse? Yes. But, instead of blaming them, I sought to understand them.

"Mom, you said that you've only been angry two times in your life, and not one of them is when you found out about Michael. Is it just too hard to go there?"

The woman who survived the Great Depression, a brother in World War II, and an alcoholic father's gambling, uttered, "Yes, I guess that's it."

I could spend my life holding a grudge for her not being able to show anger and be apologetic in the way I do, but we are two different people.

My mom says sorry with her actions every time she edits my work, strives to get me a speaking engagement, or helps our mission financially. I also believe this allows her to work through her pain and anger. Years later, while reading my manuscript, she said, "Did I ever say, 'I'm sorry'?"

"No."

"I am sorry."

"I know."

Enough said!

My dad speaks through tears every time he attempts to tell people about my mission. I recognize this as his apology.

None of us can take back the events that led to the abuse; we can only make a difference in today.

Today, I choose to break out of normal perceptions! I choose not to blame my parents. Only Michael and Gayle orchestrated my molestation. I choose not to blame the entertainment industry. While I had some exposure to sexual images on the set, the obsession with sexuality came directly from my sexual abuse. Acting actually became the place I felt safe and found purpose. I am choosing to back up and realize that authentic beauty comes out of depravity and imperfection. My relationships with my parents and others are much deeper, because of this process. I have gained an amazing perspective through walking this path. Healing is a process that uses our brokenness to evolve a breakout beauty.

Instead of defining myself by my brokenness, I decided to use my brokenness for greatness. Instead of being content with good, I needed to strive for great. Breaking out of the cocoon that I had been imprisoned in for years, I anticipated the beauty that would break forth. I would bring forth the beauty of a butterfly as I developed through this metamorphosis. Sometimes, I would experience the pain of the process. People might hurl insults out of misunderstanding. They may be in a different stage or choosing a different path, but this is my path.

I realized that my former, fellow actor actually gave me a compliment. "You have the most impenetrable shield I have ever seen." He could not admire the strength that had developed in me. I proudly wear that armor. I put on a shield of faith. This equips me to extinguish flaming arrows of those who seek to destroy me. If I consider myself valuable, I deserve protection. I am in the midst of a battle. Many people don't want the truth surrounding sexual abuse to be revealed. I need to be durable in the midst of conflict.

Part of this tenacity began in my small group of Michael's "victims." We grappled with who we were. Were we victims? Were we survivors? What were we?

We were fed up with the term "victim." So, we batted options back and forth, trying to define ourselves.

I said, "Well, we're all a bunch of brats!" We laughed at the determined spirit we all demonstrated and the courageous attitude we exhibited when we were in Michael's home. I then coined our identity, "We're The BRAT Pack!" We wanted to be different from other groups. We didn't want to be professional victims who had jumped from one group to another, seemingly just to have a new group of sympathetic ears. We didn't just want to be survivors. We did not want to go on without end. We wanted freedom from the entrapment in which we had been shackled. We did not want to focus on our victimization. At the same time, we wanted to do more than just survive. We longed to live! We desired to fight back with joint force, desiring to understand what took place in the past and how to live above those circumstances in the future.

One of the women in our group created my membership certificate with our group's ideals and desires for change:

CERTIFICATE OF MEMBERSHIP

Be it known that

Martha Nix

Is an official member of the B.R.A.T. Pack

(Boldly Resolving Abuse Together)

As a member of the BRAT Pack you have made an important choice. BRAT Pack members are not victims, or survivors, but people who have chosen to live and to actively enter into the healing process.

As a member of the BRAT Pack you are entitled to enjoy the sense of self-worth and dignity bestowed on you by your Creator. You are encouraged to commit yourself to be fully what you are—an Image-Bearer of God.

It is to be remembered that your self-worth is a settled issue and rests in the truth of WHO YOU ARE rather than what you do. The BRAT Pack has no 'shoulds.' You are loveable and uniquely created. You will be encouraged to grow in personal ways and thus demonstrate your individual uniqueness in all that you do.

As a member of the BRAT pack your emotional and spiritual growth will be gradual and there will be times when you fail. But you will be unconditionally accepted during your process of becoming like Christ. We will rejoice together at each victory as you grow in God's love and each day become more of a feeling, thinking, choosing, creative person.

You were designed for relationship. As a member of the BRAT Pack you are entitled to fellowship openly and honestly with other BRAT Pack members who are also in process. You will find support, encouragement, and understanding as you fight your battles and walk your journey into healing.

After years of living through the healing process, I realized one of the greatest morsels in this certificate was in the name. The BRAT Pack. Victims of sexual abuse are not alone! There are a pack of us inhabiting this earth, and we have no need to hide in shame!

We have so much to give. We are unique beyond measure, and we are fabulous. We are deeper than most and we can empathize with others. We matter. Who we are is valuable and who we can become is admirable.

I believe as we come to a place of forgiveness and wholeness, we should boldly come together and determine to fight the war that is waged against children's innocence. We should use our knowledge to educate people about the ploys of pedophiles and the shortcomings in parenting that led us to our experiences.

These ideals led me to start telling my story. The summer of 2003, I first shared my story in Brazil. I talked in the public school, churches, and at concerts. "No one ever talks about this. You need to continue telling your story!" encouraged a high school teacher.

I came home and searched on-line for existing organizations conquering this topic of healing and prevention. Few sites existed.

First, I grappled with what name would intrigue people to ask questions. I chose the name A Quarter Blue, since statistically A QUARTER of children will be left BLUE from the trauma of sexual abuse.

At the time, the pink ribbon was taking off. Pink products were benefitting breast cancer education and research. I wondered if a ribbon existed for child abuse prevention. I discovered the official color was established by a grandmother who lost her grandson, Michael "Bubba" Dickinson, to the effects of physical abuse. His body was left black and blue. Grandma Bonnie Finney started with one blue ribbon on her car's antenna, and now the blue ribbon is nationally recognized.

I continued to research. April had been established as the month for child abuse prevention. I had very little money, so had to be strategic on how to develop awareness of the statistics of sexual abuse through marketing. STICKERS!!! I could print 500 with a reasonable investment. If 500 cars passed hundreds to thousands of people with thought-provoking messages, numerous people would be drawn to our website to discover the meaning behind the phrases—"IT happens more than you think," "Communication—The Key to Prevention," "Truth Changes Lives," and "Build Bold Boundaries." When visitors arrived to our website they would receive helpful hints. I was giddy with excitement and anticipation ... until I found I couldn't give them away. People would avoid our booth at flea markets.

I knew that sexual abuse was a taboo subject, but I had no idea how taboo.

Every day I think about how to open more doors for the message of prevention and healing. I know our society remains undereducated. As long as we stay silent about the truths surrounding sexual abuse, we risk much. Children are in greater danger. Pedophiles are given more freedom. Survivors of this horrific crime feel alone and needlessly shamed. These facts keep me persevering. In 2007, I filed for A Quarter Blue's non-profit status. Many people counseled me that this would give us credibility and allow us to receive tax-deductible funding through donations and grants. I am thankful we made that step. However, the obstacles remain. Groups will schedule a talk, then get cold feet. People freak out for various reasons. They are afraid their child will be molested if they educate them about sexual abuse. Parents continue to squirm about having the "icky" talk with their children. If we could only live in the reality that education is empowerment and the truth will set us free!

I remind myself—be faithful to my mission and purpose. I try to focus on the victories! Hearing stories of saved lives and changed lives, encourages my soul and allows me to know I am doing what I am called to do. There have been many times that I analyze challenges to scrutinize if I am out of God's will, but He sends me affirmation to press on. I am thankful I can recognize that endurance develops perseverance and character.

I admire people who face their fears and challenges with passion. When they emerge from the rubble, they use their experiences to make a difference in the world because of what they were allowed to endure.

As survivors of sexual abuse, we must keep our eyes on the finish line of each race. Once we cross the finish line of one goal, we must celebrate and then shore up our defenses for the next. We need to be steadfast in keeping focused. We must remain hopeful in the process. Our passion should invigorate us to persevere. We are worth an amazingly victorious life and together we can make a difference. That's what makes life worth living—trusting that victory along the way will help you become incredible change agents. That's what being part of The BRAT Pack is all about.

CHAPTER ELEVEN

The Unmasked Warrior

"YOU ARE YOU!"

"You are you!" read the thankful gram sent to me from a parent of one of my students for Thanksgiving. I read it again and again, "You are you!" So, was that a back-handed compliment? It took me a good day of hearing those words replay in my head over and over, to be able to receive them as a statement of praise. "You are you!" I found myself so paranoid about those words, that I missed the next line, "Thank you for being a great influence on my kids!" I wish I could have initially received those words as they were intended, but my insecurities blinded me to the true message. I now realize I love that message! "You are you!" "I am me!" I don't want to be a counterfeit or a cast image pushed through an assembly line of masked perfection and likeness.

When I shield myself with a protective armor for the battle of healing, I must not put on the mask of insincerity—the china doll face of my childhood. I don't want to be like many victims of sexual abuse, who are masters of façades. I want to be proud of being me. The word façade holds various meanings, which illuminate the need for us to shed it. In English, it literally means the face of a building. In French, it translates to "face." In Arabic, it represents something rotting or bad. Each of us dons a mask to cover our faces or even save face at some point in our life. We may be masking raw emotions. We may be hiding behind lies. We may be hoping to mask personal flaws. We must embrace the Arabic language's translation of façade. If we live behind a façade, we will rot from the inside out. It is bad to attempt to diminish who you are by hiding behind a mask.

Do I hope that no one will notice this is not who I really am? Or am I longing for someone to give me the freedom to let my guard down? I want each victim of pain and deceit to be free today. I want to encourage each reader to say with resounding confidence, "I am Me!" "Today is the day!" It is unimportant what we are hiding; the mask needs to come off. I realize you put the mask on to camouflage a perceived ugliness with something you believe to be beautiful. Unless it is truly you, it is not a genuine beauty. Put the mask on the wall as a reminder of the entrapment you evolved out of through hard work and transparency. Express your uniqueness from behind the mask. You exist in your greatest glory when you step out from the plastered smile and isolated plastic.

Art history demonstrates this concept well. Greeks were masters at stone sculptures, and Romans tried to duplicate this art form, but didn't have the same ability to find the strength in the stone. Roman statuaries tended to crack. In order to pull off the masquerade, Romans would fill the cracks with wax in order to appear perfect. The challenge came when the pieces were placed in beautiful outdoor gardens and the sun's rays beamed down on these "masterpieces." The heat began to melt the wax that hid the cracks, and the frauds were exposed. This is how the word *sincere* originated. *Sine* means without, and *cere* means wax. We need to be sincere, for we are amazing treasures that will be placed into the heat of life. We must strive to be genuine works of art, so that when the heat is turned up, we don't melt under pressure.

A false face will oppress our process. Do not grow weary of fighting the good fight and pursuing authenticity. The rewards far outweigh the alternative of being a counterfeit. We need to strive for authenticity in who we are and how we interact with others.

While I am passionate about connecting with people who have been victimized by sexual abuse and stopping the cycle of abuse, I am so much more. I seek balance in my interaction with others. In teaching and developing relationships with children and teens, I love to pour in hope, love, and encouragement. I want them to know that they do not need to seek love in all the wrong places, and that they have someone who will shoot straight with them, all-the-while loving them. I continue to develop my gifts that have sustained me over the years. Acting, singing, and dancing were the antidote to much of my pain. I use this creativity to reach out to others. Three years ago, two of my nieces and I developed a nail campaign during April—Child Abuse Prevention Month. This is a light-hearted, creative way to help people become aware of the issues surrounding this crime against children. More often than not, people will say, "Cute blue polish." This opens a door to tell others about A QUARTER of children being left BLUE from the trauma of sexual abuse if we remain undereducated. A Quarter Blue also sponsors an Art Exhibit to awaken people to the process of healing. Singing allows me to reach out to others every Sunday, hoping that the songs will touch their hearts and allow them to be carried through the week, no matter what they encounter. It is out of my brokenness that I sing and lead others to express themselves through the arts.

My true purpose in life is to live out of my broken experiences, not be weighed down or embarrassed by the harsh realities I endured. The strings of manipulation have been severed; I will live a life of truth and freedom. I will not focus on "What if I had never been sexually assaulted? What if I had told my parents? What if ... What if ... What if ...?" I will be committed to looking forward, and to how, as I change myself, I am more empowered to be a positive change agent in our world. Join me in my fight. We must fight for ourselves, for the innocent children we want to protect in the future, and the innocent children in ourselves that we were unable to protect during our childhood.

I would never wish sexual abuse on anyone, but I do not resent going through those scary, silent years. I am thankful I am one who will not shy away from constant barriers about sharing the truth of sexual abuse. I continue to learn perseverance.

Just because I was sexually abused and refuse to keep it quiet, I am not one to be avoided or silenced. I speak for the fearful, the shamed, and innocent. Admittedly, I am stained; not only by the effects of abuse and the memories of an innocence lost, but now I am often scorned by a society that does not know how to filter through the truths I represent. I speak out about the staggering statistics, and how each one of us is affected by this epidemic of childhood sexual abuse by people we know and trust. I am committed to this cause and use every opportunity I can find to educate the public—I will persevere.

Throughout my crusade to educate society about molestation realities, I have encountered ongoing opposition and flippancy, but I refuse to stop. I will persevere. While I am baffled by people's responses—I will persevere. While I am sometimes infuriated by slammed doors and truths resented—I must persevere even more.

When someone does not understand my willingness to forgive—I will persevere. This is *my* life and these are *my* choices. I want to move forward. I do not want to keep my mind chained to the past. This freedom will better equip me to pay it forward.

As a survivor of sexual abuse, as a BRAT who wants to use my story and unique wisdom and insight, I must persevere. Each of us needs to see how we must persevere through the internal voices of doubt or discouragement. We each need to determine that our lives were meant to evolve, not dissolve. If we stifle the truth of our experiences, we potentially allow other children to have their innocence stolen by the predators living among us.

With over 41 million victims living in the United States alone—I cannot be bound to my past, or my perpetrator, or the lies that try to manipulate my life. I am worth authentic love, an experiential freedom, and an abundant life, with cracks and all. I am not a china doll, fragile in the hands of others. I am a survivor who bruises, yet heals. I am not part of the domino effect, where if something knocks me down, my world comes crumbling down. I am a pillar of strength, who will overcome. I am not a puppet, reliant on others to make my every move. I am a BRAT, one who BOLDLY RESOLVES ABUSE TOGETHER. I am breaking free from a fragile shell that sits on a shelf while life passes by. I am removing the mask that blinds others to an authentic me, and that obscures my view of the world before me. I am shattering the presumption that to be cute, cuddly, and silent is who I am supposed to be. My secret is out. "I am me!"

I am to breathe. I am to believe. I am to be! As I live off of the shelf, free from the plastic shields of sitting pretty, I can change the world. That is why I proclaim with a resounding voice, "You are not alone!" To the one feeling alone in the secret world of molestation, I cry out, "You are not the only one!" And to the one feeling frightened and broken beyond repair, I promise, "There is hope for you!" Beauty will emerge out of your brokenness!

Yes, I was abused, but I am no longer a victim. I am a warrior! I am on a mission to educate, protect, and empower. My dream is that there will one day be a shift in the tide; a turning of the minds, when people will come alongside the TRUTH and embrace it as a lifeline. I dream this not for me, but for the countless children who can be saved.

Join the battle! Join The BRAT Pack! Step off the shelf and into the battle! You are worth the fight! You are you! You are worth it! Your secret deserves to be heard! The TRUTH will set you free!

Endnotes

1. Ann Omley, "The Wise Man and the Foolish Man" (c. 1948)

2. Author Unknown, "Silversmith" (Date Unknown)

Nail Campaign Poster 2010

THERE'S POWER IN THE POLISH!

A Quarter Blue 95% of sexual assault is preventable through education, so start talking about ways to protect children from this insidious crime.

Educating ~ Protecting ~ Empowering

MAKE A STATEMENT!

During April wear blue-colored nail polish to bring attention to Child Abuse Prevention month.

A Quarter Blue: *Educating-Protecting-Empowering*
Visit www.aquarterblue.org to access tools for prevention.

Nail Campaign Poster 2011

All proceeds from the sale of *My Secret Life* will go toward
A Quarter Blue's work to stop childhood sexual abuse through
education and encourage survivors to begin the process of healing.

For additional information or to make a tax-deductible contribution
to support the work of A Quarter Blue:

A Quarter Blue
146 South Main Street L235
Orange, CA 92868
www.aquarterblue.org
714-932-0845

Stopping Childhood Sexual Abuse